THE PROSPECTS OF INDUSTRIAL
CIVILIZATION

BOOKS BY BERTRAND RUSSELL

INTRODUCTION TO MATHEMATICAL PHILO-
    SOPHY   *Second Impression, 12s. 6d. net*

THE ANALYSIS OF MIND
                    Second Impression, 12s. 6d. net

OUR KNOWLEDGE OF THE EXTERNAL WORLD.
    As a Field for Scientific Method in Philosophy
                                    8s. 6d. net

PRINCIPLES OF SOCIAL RECONSTRUCTION
    Seventh Impression, cloth, 5s. net; limp cloth, 3s. 6d. net

ROADS TO FREEDOM: Socialism, Anarchism and
    Syndicalism
        Fourth Edition, cloth, 5s. net; limp cloth, 3s. 6d. net

FREE THOUGHT AND OFFICIAL PROPAGANDA.
                    Cloth, 2s. net; paper, 1s. net

THE PRACTICE AND THEORY OF BOL-
    SHEVISM   *Second Impression, 6s. net*

THE PROBLEM OF CHINA   *7s. 6d. net*

THE PROSPECTS
OF INDUSTRIAL
CIVILIZATION

BY

BERTRAND RUSSELL

IN COLLABORATION WITH

DORA RUSSELL

LONDON: GEORGE ALLEN & UNWIN LTD.
RUSKIN HOUSE, 40 MUSEUM STREET, W.C. 1

First published in 1923

Printed in Great Britain by
UNWIN BROTHERS LIMITED, THE GRESHAM PRESS, LONDON AND WOKING

PREFACE

THE notion of writing this book arose out of two separate experiences of Bolshevik Russia in the summer of 1920, when communism was still strong and uncompromising; and of a mutual journey to China undertaken immediately after the Russian experience. Bolshevik Russia has never failed to produce a violent reaction in the spectator, either of enthusiasm or of hatred. The authors of this book, after independent observation, for they never met in Russia, were fortunate in that the fury led them in completely opposite directions, the one recoiling in disappointment, the other expanding in the delight of fresh hope and knowledge. To examine these two curiously opposite conclusions, both vehemently held, was the occupation of the six weeks journey to the East, and of the months of quiet which the gentle atmosphere of China afforded. As discussion became less inflammable, it began to appear that the chief basis for dislike was the growth of a new synthesis or orthodoxy, that sought to impose itself—in the case of the Westerner—on minds accustomed to a tradition of freedom in speech and action, and—in the case of the Russian—on characters nurtured, it is true, in a tyrannous orthodoxy, but one which was human and divine, irregular, without the clockwork discipline of the new industrial faith. Delight and enthusiasm, on the other hand, had been caused by the sight of the bare bones of modern existence, the skeleton of the philosophy underlying industrial life. The Bolshevik synthesis, though crude, suggested, by its abandonment of all traditional beliefs, the prospect of a new harmony between thought and daily life. Here in Russia, it seemed, as nowhere else in the world, existed the conception of a modern civilization.

We concluded, as some writers in Germany and Czecho-Slovakia have also concluded, that the important fact of the present time is not the struggle between capitalism and socialism, but the struggle between industrial civilization and humanity. A new economic mode of existence brings with it new views of life which must be analysed and subdued if they are not to dominate to the exclusion of human values. Thus in the past, it has been necessary to destroy a superstitious reverence for agriculture, which dominated before it was made to serve the needs of human beings. Many prejudices still held by modern people are nothing but remnants of the agricultural, or even of the hunting, stage of man's development. We came to believe that the important differences in the modern world are those which divide nations living by industrialism from those which still live by the more primitive methods, though these are being rapidly abandoned, and industrialism is spreading all over the globe. This view was reinforced by the spectacle of a non-industrial country such as China. It was helped also by the extreme similarity between the Bolshevik commissary and the American Trust magnate; both appeared as persons imbued with the importance of mechanism for its own sake, and of their own position as holders of the key to the clockwork.

As persons of a sceptical and analytic disposition, and as heretics, not to industrialism, which we regard as practically inevitable, but to a mechanistic conception of society, we set ourselves the task, first, of analysing the various forces in modern life in relation to their historical background; and second, of trying to see what ends mechanism, unsuperstitiously used, could be made to serve. The book thus falls into two parts, of which the first is analytical and the second ethical. The war has taught most intelligent people that the greatest problem of the future is the adjustment of mechanical organization to minister to individual freedom and happiness. Herd instinct—relic of a more barbaric phase—has to be diminished and herd complexes dissolved without dissolving the organization of life that has been the means of increasing comfort and intelligence. The chief enemy is always premature synthesis : whether based on traditional superstition, or on outworn instinct, or on incomplete scientific knowledge. To point to this ruthlessly wherever it is perceived, regardless of possible inconsistencies or disappointed ideals, must be the task of disinterested inquirers in any period of history.

This book is so much a product of mutual discussion that the ideas contained in it can scarcely be separately assigned.

B.R.
D.R.

Carn Voel, Treen, Penzance,
May 10, 1923.

CONTENTS

PART I

CHAPTER I

CAUSES OF THE PRESENT CHAOS

I

THE movement of human society, viewed throughout the period known to history, is partly cyclic, partly progressive ; it resembles a tune played over and over again, but each time louder and with a fuller orchestration than before. In this tune there are quiet passages and passionate passages ; there is a terrific climax, and then a time of silence until the tune begins again. Such a climax is exemplified by the period through which we are now passing or about to pass. If we think only of the one tune, it seems to end in nothingness ; if we think only of the cycle, it seems that the whole process is futile. It is only by fixing our attention upon what is progressive, upon what distinguishes one cycle from the next, that we become aware of the advance made from age to age, and of the steady movement underlying the back-and-forth eddies of the surface.

The ancient empires of Egypt and Babylonia were swept away by the Persian empire, the Persian by the Macedonian, the Macedonian by the Roman, the Roman by the Teutons and Arabs, the Arabs by the Teutons. At each stage a civilization which had reached a certain height and then grown decrepit was destroyed, and a new one built upon its ruins, sometimes only after a considerable period of chaos. Our own civilization appears to be growing decrepit and ready to fall. In all this we see only the cyclic movement of history : birth, growth, decay and death, in empires and civilizations as with the beasts of the field.

But when we compare any one of these civilizations with its predecessors, we become aware of a definite advance, particularly in two respects : first, the increase of knowledge ; and secondly, the growth in the extent of organizations, more particularly of States. From past progress in these two respects a definite though perhaps not very immediate hope for the future is seen to be justified.

The increase of knowledge and the growth of States are both sources of evil as well as of good : science has made war more destructive and large empires have made it more widespread. But although both are capable of doing harm, both are indispensable conditions of vital progress. With regard to knowledge this may perhaps be taken as obvious. With regard to the growth of States, the view that it is to be regarded as desirable results from considering the chaos in the world and the only possible ways of amending it. The only ultimate cure for war is the creation of a world-State or Super-State, strong enough to decide by law all disputes between nations. And a world-State is only conceivable after the different parts of the world have become so intimately related that no part can be indifferent to what happens in any other part. This stage has now been reached. Until recent times the Far East had no vital relation to Europe. Until Columbus, America was isolated. Until Peter the Great, Russia had little connection with the Western Powers. The late war, by its

universality of destruction, demonstrated the solidarity of mankind. And this solidarity has resulted
from industrialism and mechanical inventions, both
of which are products of science. It is science,
ultimately, that makes our age different, for good
or evil, from the ages that have gone before. And
science, whatever harm it may cause by the way, is
capable of bringing mankind ultimately into a far
happier condition than any that has been known
in the past.

On these broad grounds, optimism as to the ultimate
issue of the present chaos seems to be justified.
Meanwhile the state of the world is frightful, and is
only too likely to become worse in the near future.
If we would act wisely in this time of darkness, if
we would take our share in making the destruction
as small as possible and the new construction as
swift and solid as it is capable of being, it is necessary
that we should face all that is discouraging in the
present and all the dangers of the near future ; it
is necessary that we should diagnose fearlessly,
without regard to party shibboleths or to the desire
for the easy consolation of fallacious hopes. It is
necessary to apply in our thinking the best science
and the most enlightened ideals that our age affords.
Above all it is necessary to avoid the discouragement
and sense of impotence that are too apt to result from
the spectacle of apparently irresistible forces arrayed
against the ends which we wish to see realized. For
this purpose it is well to remind ourselves that political
forces are not strong except when they rest upon
popular support, and that, in the main, only ignorance secures popular support for what is evil. Amid
the myths and hysterias of opposing hatreds it is
difficult to cause truth to reach the bulk of the people,

or to spread the habit of forming opinions on evidence rather than on passion. Yet it is ultimately upon these things, not upon any political panacea, that the hopes of the world must rest.

Reason and the scientific temper of mind are more necessary to the world than they ever were before, because all the creeds and habits which reposed upon irrational authority have broken down. Taboos, religious beliefs and social customs are the source of order among uncivilized tribes, in so far as any order exists among them ; and they remain the source of order through successive stages of culture, until at last the sceptical intellect shows their absurdity. This happened in Athens at the height of its political and cultural glory, and in the resulting chaos Athens perished. It happened in Italy at the end of the fifteenth century, and Italy became enslaved to the fanatical Spaniards. It is happening now to the whole civilized world : the old bonds of authority have been loosed by the war, men will no longer submit merely because their forefathers did so, a reason is demanded for abstaining from claiming one's rights, and the reasons offered are counterfeit reasons, convincing only to those who have a selfish interest in being convinced. This condition of revolt exists in women towards men, in oppressed nations towards their oppressors, and above all in labour towards capital. It is a state full of danger, as all past history shows, yet also full of hope, if only the revolt of the oppressed can result in victory without too terrible a struggle, and their victory can result in the establishment of a stable social order.

What are the forces which are shaping the world and producing its struggles ? What are their relative strengths, and what are the prospects of their war-

fare ? I wish to consider these questions dispassion-
ately, not as one of the fighters, but as a scientific
investigator.

There are in the world growing forces and diminishing forces. Among the latter some still remain very
potent, but their heyday is passed, and they are
doomed (if civilization escapes disaster) to dwindle
more and more. Among the growing forces, two
stand out pre-eminent among all others, namely,
Industrialism and Nationalism. Behind both of
these, non-political itself, yet controlling all political
occurrences, is Science.

Industrialism and Nationalism both have two
forms, one for the holders of power, the other for
those who are struggling to emancipate themselves.
Capitalism and Socialism are the two forms of
Industrialism ; Imperialism and the attempt to
secure freedom for oppressed nations are the two
forms of Nationalism. Freedom for oppressed nations
is what President Wilson endeavoured to make
popular under the name of " self-determination."
The victors in the war decided that this principle
should only apply in favour of those oppressed by the
enemies of the Entente ; those oppressed by the
Entente are held to have no right to national independence. The principle of self-determination has
therefore been taken up by the Russians as regards
territories held by their enemies, and it has thus
come into a practical alliance with Socialism. But
it belongs to an entirely different order of thoughts
and sentiments, and can never have more than an
external alliance with principles so essentially international as those of Karl Marx.

We have thus four great political forces in the
world : the two forms of Industrialism, namely,

Capitalism and Socialism; and the two forms of Nationalism, namely, Imperialism and Self-Determination. The chaos in the world takes the form of a titanic conflict between these forces: Capitalism and Imperialism on one side; Socialism and Self-Determination on the other.

II

The bitterness of political and military conflict has concealed from the world and from the combatants themselves how much there is in common between the two forms of Industrialism, and also between the two forms of Nationalism. It is necessary to understand these affinities of rival forces if we are not to go astray in our attempts to analyse the present situation.

First of all, let us be clear as to what we mean by Industrialism.

Industrialism is essentially production (including distribution) by methods requiring much fixed capital,[1] i.e. much expenditure of labour in producing implements for the production of commodities which satisfy our needs and desires. It is an extension of the habit of using tools. The man who first thought of ploughing the soil before sowing took the first step towards industrialism: a plough is something which does not in itself satisfy any of our needs or desires, but diminishes the amount of labour required for satisfying our hunger. Industrialism is the extension of this practice of making tools, until the tools grow into modern machinery, which requires

[1] Capital is not money, but means of production. Money can buy capital, and is normally so employed when it is invested, but capital consists, not of money, but of such things as machinery, railways, ships, etc.

for its production and use the co-operation of large numbers of workers. As an example of industrial methods of production, we may take railways. A railway requires a very great amount of labour for its construction, yet when constructed it does not, of itself, enable us to gratify any of our wishes. We cannot eat it, or clothe ourselves with it, or sleep on it (without imminent risk of death). A railway cannot advantageously be consumed, like a loaf of bread ; it can only be used, i.e. employed as a means of providing loaves of bread, and other consumable commodities, with less labour than would otherwise be necessary. While the railway is being built, and until it is actually used, those who construct it cannot be kept alive by their own labour, which produces none of the necessaries of life, but must be supported out of the surplus of necessaries produced by other people. Consequently every increase of industrial capital involves a momentary diminution in the satisfaction of wants ; a community which is becoming industrialized is constantly forgoing the present satisfaction of wants for the sake of greater satisfaction in the future.

It is obvious that industrialism demands certain qualities in a community which is to practise it successfully. First, there must be a possibility of obtaining large organizations of workers devoted to a common task ; a railway, for example, cannot be built by one man or one family. Next, there must be, in those who can direct the labour of the community, a willingness to forgo present gratifications for the sake of greater wealth later. Thirdly, there must be a sufficiently orderly and stable government to render it highly probable that those who make this postponement will be able to reap their reward; otherwise everybody will adopt the maxim " let us eat and drink, for to-morrow we die." Fourthly, there must be a large number of skilled workers, because many of the processes of industrial production are difficult. Lastly, there must be a body of scientific knowledge, to make and utilize mechanical inventions. This last condition is the most essential of all : its absence in former times is the reason why industrialism is a recent growth.

It seems almost inevitable that, when a country is in the early stages of industrialism, the economic organization should be oligarchic, and the bulk of the population should be very poor unless it is possible to borrow extensively from more advanced countries. To take first the question of poverty : when a country has not yet become industrial its methods of production are not highly efficient, and do not, in general, produce any very great surplus above what is needed for subsistence. The first effect of a movement towards the development of industry in such a country is to take a number of workers away from work which is immediately productive, and to cause them instead to build railways or construct machines or export their produce to other countries where machines can be bought or such things as steel rails manufactured. The result is that, at first, there is a diminution in the amount of consumable commodities to be distributed. As there was already not much to spare (owing to the country having been hitherto unindustrial), the result of a diminution is apt to be serious poverty for the ordinary worker. The only way to avoid this is to industrialize very slowly, or to borrow heavily from economically more advanced countries. The latter is the expedient usually adopted when the relations with advanced countries are friendly. But when, as in Soviet Russia, borrowing is impossible owing to hostility, there remains only the alternative of great poverty or very slow industrialization.

It is even more inevitable that the economic organization of industry should be oligarchic in a country which is in the early stages of industrial development. In Great Britain, which is the oldest of the industrial countries, there is a powerful movement for self-government in industry, a movement which deserves the fullest sympathy. This is the form of socialism which has most vitality and force among British trade unionists. But in Russia, though a similar movement existed in 1917 and 1918, it has now been completely suppressed by the authorities, who have restored one-man rule in factories and the undemocratic control of all industry from above. This difference has caused a certain wholly unnecessary division of opinion : Russian communists and their adherents in the West consider Russian experience conclusive against self-government in industry, at any rate for the present, while those who adhere to ideas more akin to syndicalism find themselves impelled, in this respect, to criticize what the Bolsheviks have done. For my part, I consider the difference between English and Russian socialism as regards self-government a necessary result of the different stages of industrial development in the two countries, and I think this would have been evident to all if the habit of thinking in terms of political battle-cries had not obscured what should have been obvious facts. Self-government in industry seems to me plainly impossible in a country as undeveloped as Russia, but nevertheless perfectly possible in England. I will try to make it clear why this must be the case.

To begin with, as we have already seen, the industrializing of an undeveloped country, when it cannot be effected by borrowing, involves considerable hardship for the average working man, over and above what he suffered before the growth of industry began. If the average working man has economic control, he will resent this increased hardship, and will not be reconciled to it by the promise of ultimate benefit to his children or grandchildren. In the early days of the industrial revolution in England gangs of working men broke up the machinery of the mills, because machinery produced the same output with less labour, and therefore threw men out of work. If working men had had control of methods of production in those days the industrial revolution could never have taken place.

But it is not only the temporary increase of poverty that makes self-government in nascent industry impossible. It is also—and this is the more important reason—because when industry is new men have not the habit of co-operation in large groups of producers. Non-industrial production is an individual affair, or an affair of a family or a small group of handicraftsmen. There do not exist the customs which would facilitate voluntary combination of hundreds or thousands of workmen. An organization of a new kind is very rarely created voluntarily. It is possible by means of power to compel a number of people to work together for a common end imposed from above, not chosen by themselves ; and when they have the habit of such work, and the experience of its usefulness, they can carry it on without external compulsion. This has been the case in politics : only where kings have first produced a strongly knit State has democracy subsequently proved successful. I do not except the United States from this rule, because the political habits of the Fathers of the Constitution were those that had been formed in England in the seventeenth century. And I do not believe that an international world-State will ever prove effective except through the domination of one State or of some close alliance of States. When once the necessary organization exists, and habits of working within it have been formed, self-government becomes possible, and freedom can be gradually achieved. So it is in industry : whether nominally capitalistic or communistic, nascent industry must be more or less despotic, the despot being in one case a capitalist, in the other a State official. All the experience of the Bolsheviks bears out this view, and I have no doubt that it will prove equally true in India, China and other undeveloped countries.

It follows from these considerations that the practical difference between capitalism and socialism is not so great as politicians on both sides suppose. Certain features will appear in the early stages of industrialism under either system ; and under either system certain other features will appear in its later stages. Russian industry under the Bolsheviks reminds one of English industry a hundred years ago : long hours, a sweated wage, prohibition of strikes, absolute submission of the workers to the captains of industry, are all features which the two have in common, and must have in common, since both are attempts to develop industry without the help of foreign capital.

It follows also that the good things at which socialism aims can only be achieved where industry is highly developed and has sunk deep into the habits of the nation. In England or America, socialism, if it could be achieved without prolonged war and industrial dislocation, could bring a very considerable degree of material well-being to the whole population, by exacting only four or five hours of daily labour from every adult citizen. And it would not need to be a centralized bureaucratic system, because the workers, from long practice, have come to understand the industries in which they are employed, and would be thoroughly competent to manage them themselves. A gradual approach to these benefits is possible without a catastrophic abolition of the capitalist system, and therefore without the very grave dangers to industrialism and the whole fabric of civilization which are involved in a universal class-war. But these benefits cannot be secured in a country as yet almost unindustrial, however much it may be nominally communistic, because in such a country the total produce of labour is not very much more than is needed for subsistence, and there are not, in the general body of the population, the habits, the skill or the knowledge required for a democratic control of the processes of industrial production.

If these considerations are valid, it follows that the political disputes which centre round the class conflict, important as they are, cannot prevent the still greater importance of the development of machinery, skill and industrial habits, which will determine certain broad features in the economic life of a nation whatever may be its system of distribution, and will make two backward countries, one socialistic and the other capitalistic, resemble each other more, in many ways, than either will resemble an industrially advanced country.

III

Next to industrialism, the most potent force that moulds the modern world is nationalism. Like industrialism, nationalism has two forms: one for the holders of power and the other for those who are struggling to emancipate themselves. Nationalism in the holders of power is called Imperialism; in oppressed nations it is called the principle of self-determination. As in the case of industrialism, the two forms have much more in common than they are thought to have by those engaged in the conflict between them.

But let us first be clear as to what we mean by nationalism.

Nationalism is a development of herd-instinct: it is the habit of taking as one's herd the nation to which one belongs. As to what constitutes a nation, the only thing that can be said definitely is that a nation is a group which is defined geographically. One may feel allegiance to various kinds of groups: races, religions, professions, artists, men of science, etc., etc. When a group to which men feel allegiance is geographical, it may be called a nation, and the allegiance which is felt may be called nationalism. Thus "nations" and "nationalism" have to be defined together: they are both constituted by herd-instinct directed to a geographical group. It is a characteristic of the present age that this form of herd-instinct has acquired a very marked predominance over every other. In the past, in many periods, a man's herd consisted rather of his co-religionists than of his compatriots. Marx, who regarded the history of the world as mainly a struggle between classes, the feudal aristocracy giving place to the bourgeoisie and the bourgeoisie to the proletariat, expected a man's herd-instinct to be directed rather to his class than to his nation. Hence his followers have been astonished by the patriotism of working men and cynical about the apparent patriotism of the capitalist class. "Proletariat of all countries, unite" is the Marxian exhortation to the wage-earner to transfer his herd-instinct from his country to his class. Hitherto, this exhortation has been very unsuccessful, as the late war showed; but we cannot be sure that it will remain so.

Rivalry is part of the instinctive apparatus of human nature, and as civilization advances there is a tendency for the rival groups to grow larger and larger, from families to tribes, from tribes to small nations, and from small nations to the great nations of the present day. The essence of nationalism is the sense of rivalry between one's own nation and others. This brings with it a whole train of loyalties and friendly sentiments towards compatriots, with a correlative train of hatreds and pugnacities towards the members of rival nations. A person afflicted with nationalism believes that his own country is the most civilized and humane country in the world, while its enemies are guilty of every imaginable atrocity and vileness. Since they are so vile and atrocious, while we are so civilized and humane, there is no degree of vileness and atrocity which we may not legitimately practise towards them. This is the creed of nationalism.

It is obvious that this creed is, by its very nature, founded in falsehood and leading to strife, brutality and destruction. The beliefs of a nationalist are different in every country. The Germans considered their Kultur so superior as to be worth spreading at the cost of an European war; the English, on the

contrary, consider their own so preferable to every other as to be worth propagating by the bayonet and the lash.[1] The English and the Germans did not agree with each other's opinions, though both were nationalists. There is no doubt one nation which really is as superior as each nation thinks itself ; it is, of course, that nation (whichever it may be) to which my reader belongs. But all other nations are plainly in error in adopting the nationalist creed : they ought to admit the superiority of my reader's nation, and submit meekly to its demands. But, alas ! their claim to superiority is just as stubborn as though it were well founded, just as self-assured as in case of our own *really* superior nation.

The smallness of the difference between imperialism and oppressed nationalism is seen when an oppressed nation is liberated. We may take Poland as a recent and glaring example. For a century and a half the Russians oppressed the Poles, and the Poles professed to desire nothing but freedom. The friends of freedom everywhere befriended them, and regarded them as a gallant nation incapable of inflicting upon others such tyranny as they were suffering. Yet in the very moment of acquiring their national independence they embarked upon a war of conquest against Russia, with a view to inflicting upon as many Russians as possible the pains and tortures which Poland had formerly suffered at the hands of the Tsar. There is nothing peculiar or exceptional in this behaviour ; it is the natural behaviour of any country afflicted with virulent nationalism.

[1] See, e.g. *Daily News*, January 5, 1920. *The Times*, February 22, 1923, states in a telegram from Delhi : " The Criminal Law Amend-ment Bill has been passed by the Legislative Assembly, with a trifling alteration, giving the right of appeal in whipping cases." I have in my possession photographs showing Indians being beaten into unconsciousness because we dislike their politics.

It is not merely artificial frontiers or the blunders
of diplomatists that make the evil of nationalism ;
it is not merely the fact that some nations are oppressors
while others are oppressed. This fact is, of course,
a very grave evil, but it is the inevitable outcome of
nationalist feeling in a world where a complete equilibrium of national forces is impossible to maintain.
So long as the majority of civilized mankind continue
to feel that their only social obligation is to their
own country, and that for its advancement they
are justified in inflicting any degree of damage upon
people of other countries, so long no diplomatic arrangements or political reform can produce a tolerable
world.

The principle of self-determination, although the
weaker nations appeal to it in their struggle with the
Great Powers, is not itself nationalistic ; it is rather
an endeavour to cope with nationalism from the
standpoint of an internationalist. The true nationalist
wants self-determination only for his own country,
though the need of allies may compel him to an appear-
ance of justice towards other national claims. It is
obvious that, while national feeling remains as hot as
it is at present, self-determination, if it could be
realized and enforced against the stronger nations,
would be the best possible arrangement of national
boundaries. But it is scarcely conceivable that
it should be realized or maintained while national
feeling remains what it is. At each frontier opposing
armed forces will stand glaring at each other ; trade
will be made difficult, and when it occurs will be used
to stir up national economic hatred ; at the slightest
provocation wars will break out, in which the victors
will throw the principle of self-determination to the
winds. It is not by a formula, however admirable,

that the evils of nationalism can be cured. Nor can they be cured by adopting passionately the cause of the nations now oppressed, since to-morrow they will become oppressors if our championship is successful. The only cure for the evils of nationalism is the diminution of nationalism, the diversion of men's energies and sentiments from the barren business of national rivalry. I shall return on a later occasion to the question whether and how this can be achieved. I have no doubt that it is at present the most important task which civilization has to face, more important even than the introduction of a better economic system.

I have considered in this chapter what I believe to be the two main forces by which the modern world is being shaped. I have considered each in isolation, without regard to their inter-relations. But these inter-relations are very important and very interesting. Industrialism has in various ways contributed to the growth of nationalism, while it has for the first time in history produced the technical possibility of a super-national government for the whole world. Socialism professes to be at once international and the champion of oppressed nations, while capitalism favours nationalism as a method of distracting the working man from socialistic ideas : so long as he can be kept hating foreigners, he will be less vigorous in hating capitalists. All these factors are important in considering the conflict which is threatening to destroy our civilization.

Meanwhile there are old forces from the past, decaying but still strong—such forces as handicrafts and peasant agriculture, religion and literary habits of thought. As the rival protagonists of modern ideas weaken each other by internecine combat, the old forces grow relatively stronger, and it is quite conceivable that they will be in the end the sole victors. But of all these possibilities I will treat more at length in later chapters.

CHAPTER II

INHERENT TENDENCIES OF INDUSTRIALISM

In order to understand the operation of political and economic forces, it is useful to imitate the practice of the physicist, and study each separate force in an artificial isolation. What actually happens is not, of course, what would happen if only one force were acting, but is a resultant of the effects of them all. The problem of calculating this resultant is, however, greatly simplified by the previous investigation of the tendencies of the various single forces. The effects of nationalism in isolation are too obvious to need study, but the effects of industrialism, in so far as its action is not thwarted or complicated by other factors, are less obvious, though certainly not less important if we wish to understand the modern world. Something has already been said on this subject in dealing with the causes of the present chaos, but then our discussion was merely incidental, and now it must be taken up on its own account.

As indispensable conditions for the existence of industrialism in a community we enumerated : large organizations of workers engaged upon a common task ; willingness in the directors of industry to forgo present goods for future profit ; an orderly and stable government ; skilled workers ; and scientific

3

knowledge. Assuming that the conditions for the growth of industrialism exist, we have to inquire what effects its growth is likely to have, if it is not counterbalanced by other tendencies.

Industrialism does not consist merely in large undertakings requiring a great number of workmen. The building of the pyramids was a vast undertaking, but was not industrial. The essence of industrialism is the employment of elaborate machinery and other means (such as railways) of diminishing the total labour of production. All the characteristics of industrialism are exemplified by the substitution of a bridge for a ferry, in spite of the fact that bridges existed before the industrial era. If a small number of men wish to cross a river, less labour is involved in taking them across in a boat than in building a bridge. But when very many wish to cross, the bridge involves an economy of labour, in spite of the fact that it is a much more serious matter to make a bridge than to make a boat. It is obvious also that the building of a bridge, except for military purposes, depends upon the expected preservation of some degree of law and order, both because a bridge is easily destroyed, and because, in very unsettled times, no one can spare energy or thought for objects of which the advantage is in a more or less distant future.

The essence of industrialism is the expenditure of much joint labour upon things which are not themselves consumable commodities, but merely means to the production of other things which are consumable. From this fundamental quality all the other characteristics of industrialism follow.

The first thing to notice is that industrialism makes a society more organic, in the same sense in which

the human body, which is a collection of cells, is more
organic than a crowd of protozoa each consisting of
a single cell. Each of the protozoa is capable of all
the functions required for keeping alive ; it does not
need help from the others or die because they die.
The cells composing the human body have no such
independence ; they have different functions, all
necessary or at least useful for the life of the whole ;
and when any of the organs that perform vital
functions are destroyed, the rest perish. The eyes
can only see, the ears can only hear, and so on ; an
eye or an ear severed from the rest of the body cannot
do what is necessary to keep alive as the protozoa
can. In this sacrifice of independence to co-operation
there is both loss and gain. There is loss in the fact
that the whole assemblage of cells can be killed by one
vital wound, and that therefore a human body has
a more precarious life than a crowd of protozoa.
But there is gain in the fact that, by specializing, the
several organs become capable of doing work which
no number of protozoa could do, and that the life
of a human body is thus enriched and its responsiveness
to its environment enormously enhanced. Exactly
parallel differences exist between an industrial and
an unindustrial society.

In a primitive pastora or agricultural community
each family produces all that is needed for its own
subsistence. The happiness of such a family has
been depicted by Pope in the poem beginning :

> Happy the man, whose wish and care
> A few paternal acres bound.

But it may be doubted whether Pope would really
have liked this state of affairs, since it would not
have enabled a man to live by the sale of his verses.

A society which allows of such specialization is already on the road to industrialism.

In an industrial community no man is self-subsistent; each man takes part in a process which produces a great deal of some commodity, or of some machine for making commodities, but no man produces the whole variety of commodities necessary for preserving life. Hence trading, or at any rate some form of exchange of products, is absolutely necessary to survival wherever industry exists. The man engaged in a factory has to be fed and clothed by the labour of others, and cannot even produce what is made in the factory without the machinery and the co-operation of the other workers. He has ceased altogether to be an economically independent unit. The capitalist is at least equally dependent : if men would not work for him, he would starve. Agriculture, as it becomes more scientific, shares, though to a lesser degree, in the tendencies of industry, as in the large-scale farming of the United States : it requires manures and machines which cannot be produced on the spot, but are often brought from great distances. Thus the whole community becomes knit together, so that the life of each depends upon the life of all.

Like the human body, an industrial society has its vital organs, the destruction of which paralyses the whole organism. This becomes increasingly true as industry becomes more advanced and scientific. The destruction of a power station may cause all the factories, trams, lights and electric trains of a district to cease working. This is merely an example of the universal law that what is more highly organized is more sensitive. It follows that lawlessness and destructiveness can do far more harm in an industrial community than they can where the methods of production are more primitive.

As society grows more organic, it is inevitable that government acquires more importance. The acts of individuals have more and more far-reaching effects upon others, and therefore require to be more and more controlled in the interests of the community. Hence a diminution of individual liberty and of what may be called the anarchic side of life, i.e. the side in which a man merely follows his own whims. If this side of life is to be in any degree preserved under industrialism, special measures will have to be taken to that end. But this is a topic to be discussed again at a later stage.

Against the loss of liberty due to increase of government and organization, there is to be set a gain of liberty owing to the fact that the necessaries of life can be produced with less labour than in a pre-industrial society. The desires of an individual are subject to two kinds of restraint, namely, those due to the community and those due to material conditions. Industrialism, while it tends to increase the former, greatly diminishes the latter. The restraints imposed by material conditions are primarily those involved in warding off death. Most animals, owing to lack of foresight, die by starvation. Most human beings, owing to their possession of some slight degree of foresight, succeed in avoiding this form of death. But in a pre-industrial society they only succeed, unless they belong to the rich minority, by working hard almost all their lives in the production of food and other necessaries. This work is in itself often irksome from its excessive amount, and is a complete obstacle to the realization of all desires for knowledge, beauty or enjoyment. Such desires, where industry is undeveloped, can only be indulged by the fortunate few—kings, priests and nobles. But under industrialism the production of necessaries requires only a small part of the energies of the community, all the rest being set free for the production of either leisure or luxuries—including among luxuries education, science, literature, art and warfare. Thus Man is rendered freer by industrialism, since his bondage to Nature is diminished ; but each separate man may not be freer, since there is an increase in the pressure of the community upon the individual.

This, also, is exactly paralleled by the difference between the cells of the human body and a collection of protozoa. The separate cells of the human body have far less freedom than a protozoon, since they are compelled to co-operate with the rest of the body or perish. But the body as a whole has more freedom than a protozoon, since it has more control over its environment, more delicate senses, and more elaborate habits by which to utilize the knowledge brought by the senses.

By diminishing man's bondage to Nature, industrialism has rendered physically possible many things of great value which were only very partially possible in earlier stages. The mere business of keeping alive is shared by man with the lower animals, and does not raise him above their level in any important respect. What raises him above the level of the animals is his mental capacity, which has brought with it desires that are not merely material. When men are liberated from the pressure of the struggle to obtain food, they do not all sink into sloth and idleness ; some remain active, but in the pursuit of knowledge or art or some other purely mental object. It is the work of these men that sheds lustre on mankind as a whole. To have lived a certain number of years, consumed a certain amount of food, begotten a certain number of children similar to oneself, and then died, is not the utmost of which men are capable ; yet, owing to the scant productivity of labour it was, until lately, all that most men could hope to achieve. Now, so far as physical conditions are concerned, better possibilities exist ; education and sufficient leisure could, if we chose, exist throughout the whole community, and the business of keeping alive could become an easy and unimportant part of our daily occupation.

What is called civilization may be defined as the pursuit of objects not biologically necessary for survival. It first arose through the introduction of agriculture in the fertile deltas of great rivers, more particularly in Egypt and Babylonia. Everywhere else primitive agriculture exhausts the soil and compels frequent migrations, but this was not the case in the deltas. Here the surplus food produced by one man's labour above one man's needs was sufficient to make possible the creation of a small leisured class, and it was this small leisured class which invented writing, architecture, mathematics, astronomy, and other arts essential to all subsequent civilization. Although the class that could share in civilized pursuits increased with the improvement of agriculture and the growth of commerce, it remained unavoidably small, because labour was still not sufficiently productive to create the necessaries of life except by the whole work of most of the community. Now, though the arts and sciences remain a prerogative of the few, there is no good reason why this should be the case ; it would be possible for every man and woman to have as great a share of them as he or she might desire. If every man and woman worked for four hours a day at necessary work, we could all have enough;[1] and the leisure remaining after four hours' work is amply sufficient for even the most intensive cultivation of science or art. This fact has destroyed the only strong argument that ever existed for an oligarchic organization of society, whether economic or political, and has made it almost inevitable that, if industrialism continues without disaster, its ultimate form must be socialism, which alone avoids inequalities for which the former reason no longer exists.

The desire to diffuse civilization has, it is true, played only a very small part hitherto in the development of industrialism, and it is perhaps hardly to be hoped that it will play a great part until after

[1] This is a conservative estimate, as appears from the following considerations: To begin with, shorter hours of work do not diminish output in proportion. In the first years of the war, there were long hours and much overtime, but in the later years these were largely abandoned, as they were found not to increase production. (See Charles Myers, *Mind and Work*, University of London Press, 1920, chap. ii., on this point and on the effect of fatigue generally in diminishing output.) Hitherto, every reduction in hours of work has been found to involve no diminution of output. Lord Leverhulme (*The Six-hour Day*, Allen & Unwin, 1918) maintains that, wherever much machinery is employed, the most economical number of hours is six. The evidence he adduces, together with his great experience, must be accepted as conclusive. We may therefore assume that a four-hour day would, in the absence of any other improvement, produce two-thirds of what is now produced. A very large proportion of what is now produced cannot possibly be considered necessaries. There is, moreover, great waste through competition and armaments. And a certain percentage of the population are not engaged in work at all; I am not thinking only of the idle rich, but also of the unemployed. When we take account further of the possibilities of better organization, and of the fact that, given short hours and self-government in industry, there could be no objection to a cautious introduction of the methods of scientific management, with the almost incredible saving which they render possible, it becomes clear that, without any new technical inventions, a four-hour day could easily produce at least as great a quantity of consumable commodities as are produced at present.

the establishment of socialism. There has, however, been a very considerable diffusion of civilization in industrial countries, owing to the operation of motives which were mainly economic. A man who has some education is a more efficient worker than one who can neither read nor write ; hence all industrial countries have adopted universal compulsory education. This would scarcely have been possible without industrialism, since the time of teachers and pupils could not easily have been spared from more immediately necessary work. With the coming of industrialism and the complicated processes that it introduces, universal education becomes both more possible and more obviously necessary ; increase of education may therefore be taken as one of the inherent tendencies of industrialism.

With universal education come other things of great importance. The first of these is political democracy, which is scarcely possible where the working class is uneducated, and scarcely avoidable where it is educated. By democracy I do not necessarily mean a parliamentary regime ; the Soviet system, as originally conceived, would have been quite compatible with democracy. What I mean by democracy is a system under which all ordinary men and women participate equally in fundamental political power, though exceptional people may be excluded for special reasons, such as endeavouring to upset by force the government desired by the majority. Interpreted in this wide sense, political democracy seems to be the system of government natural to an advanced industrial community, except in times of special stress such as revolution or war.

Industrialism, as we have seen, diminishes the freedom of the individual in relation to the community, but increases the freedom of the community in relation to nature. That is to say, the actions of the individual, at any rate in the economic part of his life, become increasingly controlled by the actions of the community, or by some large organization such as a Trust; but the actions of the community become less and less controlled by the primitive necessity of keeping alive. Hence individual passions, such as those which produce art and romance, tend to die out, while collective passions, such as those which produce war, sanitation and elementary education, are liberated and strengthened. Each of these deserves separate consideration.

The decay of individual passions brings with it, first of all, a diminution of individuality. In a thoroughly industrialized community, such as the United States, there is little appreciable difference between one person and another; eccentricity is hated, and every man and woman endeavours to be as like his or her neighbours as possible. Their clothes, their houses, their household utensils, are all produced to standard pattern by the million, without any of those individual differences that characterize the products of handicrafts. And it seems that the men and women wish to assimilate themselves to the articles they use by forcing upon themselves the sameness of manufactured articles, as though the Creator Himself had adopted industrial methods, and were producing men and women wholesale with the very latest machinery warranted to make each specimen up to sample.

In such an atmosphere art and romance and individual affection cannot flourish, since they involve preservation of individuality in oneself and recognition of it in others. There are other reasons also why such things decay under industrialism as it has been practised hitherto, and I will return to this topic when I come to these other reasons. But there is one point connected with the decay of romance which belongs to our present topic. The instinct for romance, when it is denied an outlet in one's own life, seeks, as instincts will, a vicarious satisfaction in imagination. Hence the passion for sensational stories, melodramas and murder cases. A lunatic who kills his wife with every circumstance of horror is a public benefactor : into a thousand tame and listless lives he introduces the imaginative satisfaction of fierce passion. Every detail in the newspapers is eagerly devoured by men who dare not, in their own conduct, depart a hair's breadth from respectable rectitude, for fear of losing their job. At the outbreak of war the delight of many of those who expect to be non-combatants has the same source : the gladiatorial show relieves the deadly monotony of the office or the factory even better than a football match or a horse race. And in spite of all knowledge to the contrary, non-combatants persist in imagining modern war on the Homeric pattern, as an affair of individual bravery and initiative, because the dreary mechanistic mass-action that constitutes the actual operations affords no outlet to the starved instinct for individual romance. This same boredom and desire for excitement does much to increase the fierceness of revolutionary movements, and to produce the preference for revolution as against more gradual and less sensational methods.

One of the most important effects of industrialism is the break-up of the family resulting from the employment of women. The employment of women has two effects : on the one hand it makes them economically independent of men, so that they cease to be subject to husbands ; on the other hand it makes it difficult for them to bring up their children themselves. The tradition of the monogamic family is so strong in all the chief industrial countries that the effect of industrialism on the family has taken a long time to show itself. Even now, it has hardly begun in America, where Christianity is still not uncommon ; but throughout Europe the process of disintegration, which had already begun, has been enormously accelerated by the war, owing to the ease with which women found employment, in Government offices, in munition works, or on the land. Experience has shown that the average woman will not submit to the restraints of the old-fashioned marriage, or remain faithful to one man, when she can be economically independent. For the moment, the restraints and concealments imposed by the up-holders of traditional morality have somewhat obscured the extent of the change thus brought about. But the change will grow greater with time, since it belongs to the inherent tendencies of industrialism. In a pre-industrial community rich men held their wives as property, while poor men make them co-operators in their work. Peasant women do much of the hard work of agriculture, and working-class women have hitherto had their time fully taken up with house-hold work and the rearing of children. In this way, whether in town or country, the family formed an economic unit.

But when the woman goes out to industrial work like her husband, and the children spend most of their day at school, the economic tie between husband and wife is enormously weakened. It is probable that, with the growth of industrialism, the practice

of eating in public eating-houses will increase, and
house-work will be reduced to a minimum. The
children will have first their midday meal, and then
all meals, at school ; thus the peculiar work which
has hitherto been done by wives will cease more and
more. Under these circumstances, marriage, as it
has existed since men took to agriculture, is likely
to come to an end. Women will prefer to preserve
their independence, and not rely upon the precarious
bounty of an individual man. They will share their
children with the State rather than with a husband,
not invariably, but in a continually-increasing proportion of instances. I am not concerned to argue
whether this change is desirable or undesirable ;
I say only that it belongs to the inherent tendencies
of industrialism, and must be brought about by the
continuance of industrialism unless counteracted by
some very potent force. It has, of course, the effect,
always characteristic of large-scale industry, of increasing the pressure of the community upon the
individual. The family has been hitherto a refuge
of privacy, where it was possible to escape from the
State, and even, to a certain extent, from public
opinion. A man with unusual tastes or opinions
could bring up his children with a view to their
sharing his peculiarities ; but this must cease when
the State takes over the education of children and
(as it must ultimately do) the whole economic burden
of their maintenance. Thus the break-up of the
family must increase the tendency to uniformity
throughout the population, and weaken all those
individual traits which cannot grow or flourish in
a life lived wholly in public.

Religion, in its traditional forms, appears to be
difficult to combine with industrialism, although it

is by no means obvious why this should be the case. Of course the successful capitalists remain religious, partly because they have every reason to thank God for their blessings, and partly because religion is a conservative force, tending to repress the rebelliousness of wage-earners.[1] But industrial wage-earners everywhere tend to lose their religious beliefs. I think this is partly for the merely accidental reason that the teachers of religion derive their incomes either from endowments or from the bounty of the rich, and therefore often take the side of the rich, and represent religion itself as being on this side. But this cannot be the sole reason, since, if it were, wage-earners would invent democratic variants of the traditional religion, as was done by the English Independents in the seventeenth century and by the peasants who revolted against agrarian oppression in the Middle Ages and in the time of Luther. It is singularly easy to adapt Christianity to the needs of the poor, since it is only necessary to revert to the teachings of Christ. Yet that is not the course which industrial populations take ; on the contrary, they tend everywhere to atheism and materialism. Their rebellion against traditional religion must, therefore, have some deeper cause than the mere accidents of present-day politics.

The chief reason is, I believe, that the welfare of industrial wage-earners is more dependent upon human agency, and less upon natural causes, than is the case with people whose manner of life is more primitive. People who depend upon the weather are always apt to be religious, because the weather is capricious and non-human, and is therefore re-

---

[1] See e.g. the teachings of Hannah More and Wilberforce, as quoted in Hammond's *Town Labourer*, p. 225 ff.

garded as of divine origin. On the rock-bound coast of Brittany, where Atlantic storms make sea-faring a constant and imminent peril, the fishermen are more religious than any other population of Europe ; churches crowd the coast, particularly its most dangerous portions, while every headland has its Calvary, with the lofty crucifix so placed as to be visible from many miles out to sea. While the fisherman is at sea, he and his wife pray for his safe return ; as soon as he lands, his relief finds expression in drunkenness. A life of this kind, exposed constantly to non-human dangers, is the most favourable to traditional religion. Indeed, the whole of traditional religion may be regarded as an attempt to mitigate the terror inspired by destructive natural forces. Sir J. G. Frazer, in his *Golden Bough,* has shown that most of the elements in Christianity are derived from worship of the spirit of vegetation, the religion invented in the infancy of agriculture to insure the fertility of the soil. Harvest Thanksgiving, prayers for rain or fair weather, and so on, illustrate what has been really vital in religion. To the peasant, fertility and famine are sent by God, and religious rites exist to secure the one and avert the other.

The industrial worker is not dependent upon the weather or the seasons, except in a very minor degree. The causes which make his prosperity or misfortune seem to him, in the main, to be purely human and easily ascertainable. It is true that natural causes affect him, but they are not such as we are accustomed to attribute to supernatural agency. God may send rain in answer to prayer, because the need of rain was felt while religion was still young and creative. But although a population may be ruined by the exhaustion of its coal-fields, no one supposes that

God would create new seams, however earnestly the miners were to pray. Petroleum may bring prosperity, but if Moses had brought petroleum out of the rock instead of water, we should have regarded the occurrence as a fact of geology, not as a miracle. The fact is that religion is no longer sufficiently vital to take hold of anything new ; it was formed long ago to suit certain ancient needs, and has subsisted by the force of tradition, but is no longer able to assimilate anything that cannot be viewed traditionally. Hence the alteration of daily habits and interests resulting from industrialism has proved fatal to the religious outlook, which has grown dim even among those who have not explicitly rejected it. This is, I believe, the fundamental reason for the decay of religion in modern communities. The lessened vitality of religion, which has made it unable to survive new conditions, is in the main attributable to science. It remains to be seen whether science will prove strong enough to prevent the growth of a wholly new religion, such as Marxism, adapted to the habits and aspirations of industrial communities.

There is one other tendency which has hitherto been very strong in industrialism, but which, I believe, might cease to characterize industry under socialism ; I mean, the tendency to value things for their uses rather than for their intrinsic worth. The essence of industrialism, as we saw, is an extension of the practice of making tools. In an industrial community, the great majority of the population are not making consumable commodities, but only machines and appliances by means of which others can make consumable commodities. This leads men to become utilitarian rather than artistic, since their product has not in itself any direct human value. The man who makes a railway is regarded as more important than the man who visits his friends by travelling on it, although the purpose of the railway is to be travelled on. The man who reads a book is thought to be wasting his time, whereas the man who makes the paper, the man who sets the type, the man who does the binding, and the librarian who catalogues it, are all regarded as performing valuable functions. The journey from means to end is so long, and the distinctive merits of industrialism are so exclusively concerned with means, that people lose sight of the end altogether, and come to think mere production the only thing that is of importance. Quantity is valued more than quality, and mechanism more than its uses.

This reason, as well as the one previously mentioned, accounts for the decay of art and romance under industrialism. But the utilitarian tendency of in- dustrialized thought goes deeper than the decay of art and romance ; it upsets men's dreams of a better world, and their whole conception of the springs of action. It has come to be thought that the important part of a man's life is the economic part, because this is the part concerned with production and utilities. It is true that, at present, the economic part needs our thought, because it is diseased ; just as, when a man's leg is broken, it is temporarily the most important part of his body. But when it is healed and he can walk on it, he forgets about it. So it ought to be with the economic part of life ; we ought to be able to use it without having to think of it all day long. The bodily needs of all could be supplied, as a matter of course, by means of a few hours of daily labour on the part of every man and woman in the community. But it should be the remaining hours that would be regarded as important—hours which could be devoted to enjoyment or art or study, to affection and woodlands and sunshine in green fields. The mechanistic Utopian is unable to value these things : he sees in his dreams a world where goods are produced more and more easily, and distributed with impartial justice to workers too tired and bored to know how to enjoy them. What men are to do with leisure he neither knows nor cares ; presumably they are to sleep till the time for work comes round again.

This utilitarianizing of men's outlook is, I believe, not inseparable from industrialism, but due to the fact that its growth has been dominated by commercialism and competition. A socialistic industry could be the servant, not the master, of the community ; this is one fundamental reason for preferring socialism to capitalism. I shall have more to say on this subject at a later stage. For the present, I wish only to warn the advocates of economic reconstruction against the danger of adopting the vices of their opponents, by regarding man as a tool for producing goods, rather than goods as a subordinate necessity for liberating the non-material side of human life. Man's true life does not consist in the business of filling his belly and clothing his body, but in art and thought and love, in the creation and contemplation of beauty and in the scientific understanding of the world. If the world is to be regenerated, it is in these things, not only in material goods, that all must be enabled to participate.

CHAPTER III

INDUSTRIALISM AND PRIVATE PROPERTY

WE have considered industrialism hitherto as a technical method of production, without regard to the system of distribution, or to political conditions except in so far as they affect the mere possibility of large-scale industry. It is necessary now to undo this artificial simplification. Two institutions especially have affected industrialism profoundly, namely, private property and nationalism. Each of these two institutions has, in its turn, been greatly changed by industrialism, and the two together have become a menace to the continued existence of our civilization. I propose to consider the interactions of industrialism first with private property, and then with nationalism.

Private property, like religion, is an institution which has come down to us from the time when men first took to agriculture. Before that time, nomadic pastoral tribes possessed flocks and herds, but possession depended solely upon warlike efficiency, not upon any legal tenure. Legal tenure begins with agriculture, and applies primarily to land and agricultural produce. Private property in land existed in Babylonia in the time of Hammurabi in practically the same form in which it exists among ourselves at the present day. The essence of private property is legal possession secured to some person or group within the State, together with the rights built upon that possession. It is not essential that the possessor should be an individual. Land owned by a college or monastery is private property, just as much as land owned by an individual. Village communism, which existed throughout most of Europe in the Middle Ages and in Russia down to our own days, is to be included under private property, unless the village is an independent State. Private property exists wherever the State, by law, secures the exclusive enjoyment and use of anything valuable to an individual or to a group. Thus private property is something created by the State, and existing only where the State is strong enough to exact respect for the laws.

The power of the State rests, always and everywhere, upon armed force. A State exists only so long as it is able to repel invaders, or to find allies who will repel them. All rights of property exist only within the State, and therefore all are abrogated by foreign conquest. In this sense, private property is derived from the right of the sword. But it is only the State that depends upon the right of the sword ; the individual property-owner within the State depends upon the legal rights granted to him by the State.

The immense majority of historical and existing States owe their origin to a small group of warlike men conquering a large number of more peaceable aborigines. This has been the origin of almost all the States of Europe and North and South America, of the Semitic States of ancient and mediaeval times, and of the various monarchies of India. But great differences arise according to the relative strength and civilization of the invaders and the aborigines. In

North America and Australia, the invaders were strong enough to exterminate the aborigines, and the same thing must have occurred constantly in pre-historic times, but in historical times this case was rare in Europe and Asia. As a rule, the invaders were less civilized than the people whom they conquered, and they needed these people's labour in order to be able to enjoy the fruits of conquest. They therefore divided up the land among themselves, and made the native population into slaves or serfs. In North America and Australia, an exactly converse process has taken place after the extermination of the natives. The first comers among the white men, having seized the land, have had to attract labour from abroad, and have therefore tempted white men by high wages and brought coloured men by brute force. From our point of view, however, this does not greatly affect the question. In the newer countries, as in the older empires, the source of private property is possession of the land by a warlike minority, who can determine the conditions on which they will allow others to cultivate it.

From this system to the liberal regime of free competition, the evolution was in most countries very slow. Gradually it was discovered that the owners of the land could acquire more wealth by letting it and allowing the cultivators to own the produce than they could by standing over the cultivators with a lash. And when the aristocratic landowners lost their military supremacy, the peasants rose against them and acquired ownership of the land by the same method, namely, armed force, which had originally given possession to the nobles. Moreover, with the growth of commerce and manufacture new forms of property, not directly based on land, came into existence. It began to be thought that a man had a right to possess what he had acquired by his own industry. Thus private property began to be viewed as the reward of labour, not (as at first) as the division of the plunder by a gang of brigands. The new view increasingly prevailed, although it remained the case that many of the richest were among the idlest, confining their exertions to the receipt of rent.

There came thus to be a conflict between the liberal and the aristocratic view of property, the liberal view being based upon the right of a man to the produce of his own labour,[1] the aristocratic upon the right of conquerors and their descendants to ownership of the land. The liberal point of view, if it had been consistent, ought to have aimed at abolition of all private property in land : Henry George and the Single Taxers represent the thorough-going development of liberalism. But various difficulties prevented the success of this suggestion. In the first place, Liberalism is essentially individualistic : it considers a man as an individual producer, who has created a certain amount of wealth, to which he has a right. This outlook is antagonistic to the State, and therefore displays a reluctance to State ownership of land, which is the only alternative to private ownership. In the second place, the Liberal outlook retains a belief in the sacredness of property, and therefore cannot easily advocate confiscation of property in land. In the third place, the distinction between the landowner and the capitalist has become blurred as capitalism has developed, because most great modern capitalists derive their wealth from ownership of raw materials or of some legal monopoly. The result is that they

---

[1] This view originates with Locke's *Second Treatise on Government*, chap. v.

do not desire equal access for all to the soil and the raw materials, but find their interests bound up with those of the landowners.

But none of these things would have made Liberalism so utterly inapplicable to the modern world as it has become. This result has come from a more fundamental characteristic of industrialism, to which we must now turn our attention.

In a non-industrial community, Liberal ideals, if they could be carried out, would lead to a division of the national wealth between peasant proprietors, handicraftsmen, and merchants. Such a society exists at this day in China, except in so far as it is interfered with by foreign capitalists and native military commanders. The latter revert to the right of the sword, which belongs to an earlier stage ; the former introduce fragments of modern industrialism. But if foreign influences could be excluded and a stable government established, China could have an economic system very similar to that of France after the French Revolution had realized the liberal ideals of the physiocrats. In such a society, no one has any strong interest in abolishing private property, for, in spite of its inequalities, it is not clear that any other system would be better, and it is thought that energy and enterprise will enable any man to rise in the social scale. And although money brings advantages and pleasures to its possessor, it does not give him anything like the same power over the lives of others as is possessed by the modern capitalist. Very little wealth is required in order to become a peasant proprietor or handicraftsman, and when once this position has been achieved a man can, with reasonable good fortune, earn his living without being dependent upon any master.

But when industrialism is introduced into a community which recognizes the right of private property, a quite new situation is produced. This is due to the fact that the workers who produce capital instead of consumable commodities—for example, the men who make a railway—have to be kept alive through the slow process of production, and have to work co-operatively in large numbers. There is thus need of some authority to direct their labour, and this authority must be possessed of sufficient surplus wealth to be able to feed and clothe them throughout the time occupied by the work. Those who direct the enterprise and pay for the labour demand as their reward the ownership of the product. In this way these men become *capitalists*, i.e. owners of means of production. It follows that, wherever industrial methods prevail, no man can produce except by permission of the capitalists. They therefore acquire the power of life or death over the wage-earner, since he cannot make a living unless some capitalist chooses to employ him. We thus have the same situation in industry as exists in agriculture when the land is in the hands of great landowners.

But there is no possibility of avoiding the dependence of the wage-earner upon the capitalist by any method analogous to peasant proprietorship, because of the collective labour required for industrial undertakings. It is essential to any large industrial undertaking that all the labour should be under one management, and that the product should be under one ownership.[1] A railway, for example, could not be constructed except by a single authority, or worked if each employee were given the absolute ownership of a small portion of

[1] I mean, of course, the ownership of one corporation, not of one man.

the line, after the analogy of peasant proprietorship. The individual workman cannot, by any possible method, retain the independence of the handicrafts- man. Hence arises socialism, as a means of making the individual worker dependent only upon the community of his fellow-workers, not upon the arbit- rary will of a special set of privileged beings, the capitalists.

For this reason above all others, Liberalism, with its insistence upon the individual, is unable to find any cure for the evils of capitalism.

There are various developments connected with this fundamental difficulty, all of which reinforce the argument against any possibility of a satisfactory development of industrialism while private ownership of capital is retained. I leave out of account for the present all arguments as to the connection of capital- ism with imperialist wars, because I propose to discuss this question when I come to the inter-action of capitalism and nationalism. There is, however, a closely-allied question which belongs to our present topic, and that is, the growing connection of important capitalistic enterprises with the State.

Industrial undertakings tend to increase in size, and also derive advantage from combination, since competition cuts prices. For both reasons, the goal of all large businesses is monopoly. Trusts more and more replace that free competition which is the liberal ideal, and which America vainly strove to keep alive by anti-trust legislation. The community thus becomes dependent upon a single company for the supply of some necessary commodity. And if the commodity is one which, like steel or oil, is needed by the State in time of war, the State becomes depend- ent upon the Trust for its very existence. Thus unless the State owns the Trust, the Trust inevitably comes to own the State. This condition is most obvious in America, because America is the most advanced nation industrially. But it has come to be the case everywhere since the war. Thus we may say that, in advanced industrial countries, all big industries are already run by the State ; but we must add that the State is the Trust magnates, not the nominal government which is allowed to subsist in order to bemuse and deceive the people.[1]

It is a commonplace among socialists and syndicalists that the modern industrial State, even when it is nominally democratic, is really an organ of the capitalists. This is certainly true in fact, as is evident from the action of the State during labour disputes, particularly in the United States, where the army is employed against strikers and for the coercion of the Law Courts in cases of illegal violence on the part of capitalists. Where compulsory military service exists, as in France, strikers are mobilized and thus become subject to military law. England has not yet perfected its technique for dealing with strikers, but is likely to do so before long, and has recently passed special legislation for that purpose. Nowhere is the State neutral as between capital and labour. The excuse is the preservation of law and order. But the law is always, by its very nature, on the side of established injustice. It was the Supreme Court decision in the Dred Scott case which showed Northern Americans that slavery could not be abolished by peaceful methods. Similarly the fact that the law and the law courts consistently decide against labour is one of the most powerful arguments for revolution, and

[1] Cf. Report of Committee on Trusts (Cd 9236), 1919, reprinted 1922, especially the account of the American Meat Trust, pp. 8–10.

against those who still struggle to believe in a peaceful evolution. It is an odd fact that capitalists, while professing to dislike revolution and violence, at the same time adopt every possible device for proving to labour that no other method of advance is possible.

The reasons which lead the State to be on the side of the capitalists are many and various, in addition to those already mentioned. There are first of all reasons of mere corruption, direct or indirect. A man who has climbed into power by advocating the interests of labour finds that his income will be ten or twenty times as great if he sells those interests than if he remains faithful to his constituents ; this argument will prove convincing to many men. Then there is the more insidious influence of living a comfortable life among well-to-do people. This takes the edge off a man's protests against economic injustice, and makes him receptive of any reasoning tending to show that improvement must be slow and gradual. Then there is the psychological effect of power, tending to make a man dictatorial and executive rather than sympathetic and idealistic. Apart from these things, there is the sheer strength of the capitalists, the fact that they can produce chaos by manipulating prices, that they can blacken any man's character through their control of the Press, that they can withhold necessary supplies, and that in time of war they can cause defeat unless they are placated by enormous bribes. And those who desire a change in the social system will be regarded by all thoughtless people as more responsible for the disorder involved in the process than those who defend the *status quo*, however unjust the *status quo* may be, and however ruthless the methods by which it is defended.

Liberal ideals assumed that every man was free to

pursue his own economic interest. As a revolt of merchants and manufacturers against the old-fashioned State controlled by aristocratic landowners, Liberalism did valuable work in the eighteenth and nineteenth centuries, but its ideals have been rendered obsolete by the increase of organization which industrialism has brought about. Upholders of free competition struggled vainly against both Trusts and trade unions, which grew jointly in strength and are still growing. Individualists, having freed business from the control of the State, discovered that they had subjected the State to the control of business. Largely through the instrumentality of militarism and war, labour became more and more subject to the State, at the very moment when the State was becoming enslaved to big business interests. How far this process has gone is naïvely evidenced in a letter to various New York newspapers from Mr. A. C. Bedford, Chairman of the Standard Oil Company (Nov. 25, 1920). Speaking of Italy, he says :

Italy's principal commodity of export, labour, will in future be under Government control, and the interests of Italian emigrants to foreign countries will be more fully protected. Not only that, but it is hoped to distribute Italian labour scientifically in order that the country may receive the greatest benefits by receiving in exchange coal and other raw products of her industry. This plan will be opposed by the Socialists, who say that the Italian labourers will have no right to choose their homes, and that it may close the United States to them, as they believe this country will not permit emigrants to enter with the intention of remaining virtual nationals of the country from which they come.

We have travelled far from Liberal ideas when labour can be treated as a commodity of export to be exchanged against coal.

The class war, in one form or another, is an inevitable outcome of these conditions, unless perception of the danger promotes conciliation on both sides. We can now enumerate the factors by which it is produced :

1. Industrialism makes society more organic, and therefore increases the power of the State.

2. Industrialism gives a wholly new power over men's lives to those who control the use of capital.

3. The institution of private property, inherited from the pre-industrial era, has allowed the control of capital to be in the hands of certain private persons, the capitalists.

4. The capitalists have thus acquired control of the State with the vastly-increased powers that industrialism has given to it.

5. Meanwhile the new habits of life produced by industrialism have destroyed the traditional beliefs of wage-earners, while education has given them a new intelligence in criticising the social system.

6. Education has enabled the workers to acquire political democracy, while the plutocratic control of the State has rendered political democracy almost worthless.

7. Owing to the inevitability of large economic organizations, and to the power of those who control the use of capital, individual freedom as conceived by Liberalism is no longer possible.

8. Therefore the only way by which the communiyt can avoid being enslaved to the capitalists is the collective ownership of capital by the community, as advocated by socialism.

9. Since capitalists profit by the present system, they cannot be dispossessed except by the class war, unless the preponderance of force against them be-

comes so overwhelming that they will abdicate voluntarily.

Owing to the long tradition of private property, the opposition to it develops very gradually. By Marxian rules, the working classes ought to be all Socialists, but they are not. In so far as this is due to the influence of tradition, it is to be expected that the Marxian formula will gradually become true, because industrialism is a powerful solvent of tradition. We find, accordingly, that the number of socialists among the proletariat continually increases, and that there is little likelihood of peace in the world of labour so long as capital remains in private hands. The issue between labour and capital is obscured and complicated by nationalism, which we shall consider in the next chapter. But nationalism does not alter our main conclusion, which is, that the survival of capitalism must rouse increasing popular opposition and generate a class war which will, sooner or later, make capitalistic industry impossible. From this class war only two issues are possible in the long run : either prolonged chaos leading to the collapse of industry, or the establishment of socialism. Thus the only stable system for advanced industry is socialism.

With the greater need of organization and control resulting from industrialism, the private capitalist becomes an unduly anarchic survival, preserving for himself alone a form of liberty which the rest of the community has unavoidably lost, and which, when industry is well developed, becomes infinitely harmful to the community as a whole, through the excessive power which it confers upon a small class. Capitalism is essentially transitional, the survival of private property in the means of production into the industrial era, which has no place for it owing to the fact that production has become co-operative. Capitalism, by being ill adapted to industrialism, rouses an opposition which must in the end destroy it. The only question is whether labour will be strong enough to establish socialism upon the ruins of capitalism, or whether capitalism will be able to destroy our whole industrial civilization in the course of the struggle.

CHAPTER IV

INTERACTIONS OF INDUSTRIALISM AND NATIONALISM

INDUSTRIALISM, if it stood alone, would organize the whole world gradually as one producing and consuming unit, since it contains within itself no inherent limitation of the tendency to large-scale organizations. Industry would be practised in the regions most convenient from the proximity of power or raw materials ; the soil would be utilized, in each country, only for the crops which that country could produce best. The dependence of individuals upon the community would extend to nations : each country would produce only a small part of the commodities required for its subsistence, and would acquire the remainder by trading with other countries. This was the ideal of the early industrialists—Cobden and the Manchester School—who were all of them internationalists, and believed that industrialism would introduce a reign of universal peace.

But it is not in this direction that the world has developed or is developing. Industrialism has encountered and unintentionally fostered a force as powerful as itself, namely, nationalism, which has tended more and more to make each nation an independent economic unit. It is through the interactions of nationalism and industrialism, even more than through the conflict of capitalism and socialism, that the world is being driven back into barbarism. Unless the destructive effects of nationalism can be mitigated, there seems little hope for mankind except in a total collapse of the industrial system. The rather intricate effects which nationalism and industrialism have had upon each other are the theme of the present chapter.

Nationalism is a passion which has an instinctive root, namely, rivalry between different groups, or herd-instinct, as it is called. This instinct, like most others, has on the whole been biologically useful, but persists quite regardless of its biological utility, and operates independently of any consciousness of utility. Industrialism has rendered this instinct no longer useful, and has at the same time immensely stimulated it. To take an analogy : suppose some new diet were adopted which simultaneously strengthened men's sexual impulses and rendered women capable of parthenogenesis, we should then have the sexual instinct at once increased and rendered biologically useless. So it has been with herd-instinct under the influence of industrialism.

The operation of herd-instinct may be seen in any gregarious species of animals. Members of the same herd like to be together ; a sheep separated from the flock is unhappy until it can return. Intruders from another herd are expelled or put to death ; ants kill any ant not belonging to their own nest, if it is found in their preserves. The herd jointly exploits a certain region for food, and adopts peaceable means of distributing the food among its members. That is to say, the economic relations of members of the same herd are regulated by law. Broadly speaking, there is no fighting within the herd except between males for possession of the females at the breeding season. But if

5

a foreign animal of the same species intrudes into any place which the herd regards as its own property, the intruder is attacked, and is fortunate if it escapes with its life. Such is the herd-instinct in animals, and such it is in man.

In man the herd-instinct is very strong, and more effective than with most gregarious animals, because his intelligence facilitates more effective co-operation. In early stages, it is of great biological utility. It leads a stronger tribe to attack a weaker one, exterminate it, and appropriate the land from which its food supply was derived. The stronger tribe is thus enabled to have a larger number of descendants, and to increase its biological strength still further. It was in this way that the conquering races, such as the Aryans, the Semites, and the Chinese acquired the fertile parts of the earth's surface, and replaced the older races which must have been at one time far more numerous. The instinct of herd-solidarity and herd-pugnacity which produced these agreeable consequences was transmitted to the descendants of the conquerors, or at any rate the more successful among the descendants, since those who became less pugnacious and cohesive were in their turn slain by their more bellicose neighbours. Thus the dominant races of the present day are the outcome of a long series of selections, the survivors being on each occasion the conquerors in war, and conquest in war being mainly due to the strength and ferocity of herd-instinct. The instinctive disposition thus selected remains, though the circumstances are now wholly changed. The strength of the instinct is shown by the laudatory names we give to it, such as patriotism, public spirit, devotion to the good of the community, etc.

Various circumstances determine what collection of human beings constitutes a man's herd for purposes of herd-instinct. The main factor always is war : those who fight on the same side are the same herd. Hence, other things being equal, members of the same State tend to belong to the same herd. But the State is an artificial entity, and is often powerless to prevent the formation or perpetuation of rival herds within its borders. This happens especially when there are different races, languages and religions among the subjects of the same government. Sometimes these causes of disunion can be overcome, as in Switzerland, but this is exceptional. It is difficult to say why the Celtic Highlanders of Scotland have been successfully incorporated with the Anglo-Saxons of Lowland Scotland and England, while the Irish have remained a separate nation, although the Highlanders preserved their native language while the Irish did not. Such cases compel us to admit that the genesis of national feeling is in some degree obscure. But they are not numerically the most important cases. The great homogeneous nations, such as England, France, and Germany, which have a long national history, identity of language and similarity of manners and customs, as well as the habit of fighting in common against external enemies, have all the elements combined that go to make up national feeling. It was especially England and France that set the example of national-ism to the world ; and from them it spread to other nations, chiefly in the endeavour to resist the aggres-sions which their nationalism had inspired.

It is a mistake to suppose that nationalism is generated by an economic motive. There are groups that are held together by economic motives—for example, a gang of brigands, or the leaders of a political party. But it is not economic motives that determine what nation a man shall belong to ; this is determined by instinct or sentiment, often in opposition to economic self-interest. The British have enriched Egypt, yet Egyptian Nationalism wants to be rid of them. The Austrians enriched Trieste, which is greatly impoverished by belonging to Italy ; yet the inhabitants of Trieste wished, before the war, to become Italian. If men only wished to grow rich, or were actuated solely by economic motives, all their groupings would be like joint-stock companies, and would not have the passionate strength that belongs to national feeling. Of course, since nationalism exists, it is possible to exploit it for economic ends, just as it is possible to exploit any other human desire. Some men make money out of keeping gaming-tables, but there would be no gambling if we were all guided by economic self-interest. Similarly, some men grow rich by pandering to patriotism, but there would be no patriotism if all were guided by economic self-interest. Patriotism is part of the irrational instinctive foundation of human nature, not part of that rational pursuit of happiness which theoretically inspires the actions of sensible men.

But in saying that patriotism is instinctive we are not saying that it cannot be generated by artificial means. Just as a match-maker can cause two people to fall in love with each other, so a skilful government can produce national feeling in those who would otherwise be destitute of it. The supreme example of success in this practice is the United States. The original thirteen States had each some State patriotism, but only acquired the beginnings of collective patriotism through the War of Independence. This collective patriotism, however, was not very strong, since, if it had been, the Civil War could not have taken place. It is since the end of the Civil War that America has achieved her great triumphs in the manufacture of patriotism. In spite of an overwhelming influx of foreigners of all sorts, so that only a small proportion of the present inhabitants of the United States are descended from people living there at the time of Lincoln's death, it has yet been found possible to produce a degree of national consciousness hardly inferior to that of the oldest and most homogeneous nations of Europe. It is this intensity of national consciousness that enabled America to put forth a first-class effort in the war, and is enabling her now to make a bid for world-empire with more hope of success than attended the previous efforts of Spain or France or Germany. In view of such a remarkable achievement, those who wish to understand modern patriotism will do well to study America's methods.

It must be confessed that America had certain advantages which are denied to other nations. The immigrants were mostly destitute refugees, fleeing from poverty or oppression in their own countries— Irish, Italians, Southern Slavs, Russian and Polish Jews, and so forth. To them, safety from pogroms, with even the lowest wages paid to unskilled labour in the United States, represented freedom and comfort. America had the prestige of being called the Land of Liberty, and its government did not discriminate among different religions or different varieties of the white race. The immigrants had therefore as much reason to think well of America as they had to think ill of the governments from whose tyranny they had fled.

Nevertheless, most of them would have remained without political consciousness or American patriotism but for the influence of the schools.[1]   In the schools the children were taught to be good Americans, and to feel gratitude to the country from which they derived so many benefits.   Coming from industrially undeveloped regions, their imaginations were impressed by the material civilization of America, and they were easily led to despise the old world of Europe, with its cramped hatreds and absurd traditionalisms.   All this the schools taught to each new generation of children ; and as the number of already manufactured patriots increased, each new generation became easier to assimilate through the contagion and example of their predecessors.

The case of America may serve as an example of the effect that industrialism has had in training and intensifying the instinct out of which patriotism arises.   The operation of herd-instinct is intensified by (*a*) closeness of co-operation within the herd, (*b*) consciousness of the herd as a whole, and of outsiders, (*c*) apprehension of external dangers.   All these three factors are heightened by industrialism.   As regards closeness of co-operation within the herd, we have said enough already in previous chapters.   Consciousness of the herd as a whole, and of outsiders, is increased by railways and easy travel, by large economic groups, by contact with foreigners, but above all by education and the Press, which are the two supreme promoters of nationalism in the modern world.   The Press is, of course, dependent upon education, since it has little power where only a minority can read.   The nationalistic tone of the Press is due mainly to commercial motives, since few people

[1] A good account of the effect of American education on the children of immigrants is given in chap. vii of Colyer's *Americanism* (Labour Publishing Co., 1922).

will buy a newspaper that does not minister to their national pride. But the nationalism of education is due almost entirely to sheer instinct. Hardly any of those who direct the education of civilized countries have ever asked themselves whether any useful purpose is served by teaching the young a lot of ridiculous nonsense about the power and merits of their own country, and the weakness and demerits of its enemies. They have adopted this course instinctively, exactly as aristocrats used to teach family pride to their children. We can see the absurdity of the quarrels of Montagues and Capulets, but the quarrel of English and Germans was every bit as absurd.

How profound is the influence of education in promoting nationalism is made evident to any one who comes in contact with the peasantry of a backward country. The herd-instinct of an uneducated peasant is almost entirely confined to his own village. When his country goes to war, he is aware that the authorities do certain things, such as mobilizing the young men, requisitioning horses, and so on. But his motive in complying with such orders is the motive of obedience : experience has shown that it is dangerous to resist the authorities. Their purpose in giving orders does not concern the peasant ; he does not co-operate in the war with his will, as the citizen of an advanced country does. The difference is almost entirely due to lack of education. A man who knows no history or geography cannot conceive his nation as an entity unless he is in constant contact with foreigners, which will not be the case with the peasant in the interior of a large undeveloped empire. In small countries, such as the Balkans, intense patriotism is possible without education, especially where villages of different nationalities exist side by side. For in that case village patriotism, always easy to primitive villagers, is naturally combined with national patriotism. Neighbouring villages are in a state of feud, ready to destroy each other on the slightest provocation ; and in their feuds other villages of the same race are their natural allies. But in the interior of large homogeneous empires, where no enemy is visible, this state of ferocity and hatred can only be produced artificially. The more or less unconscious purpose of our education is to produce it ; and everywhere education is successful in this purpose.

Apprehension of external dangers is greatly increased by industrialism, for two reasons. On the one hand, education and the Press increase the awareness of dangers that do exist, and the fear of imaginary dangers invented by militarists to terrify poltroons. But on the other hand, the actual dangers, not only the fears of them, are multiplied a thousandfold by industrialism, which increases the destructiveness of weapons of war, and the proportion of the population that can be set apart for making and wielding them. This is a commonplace ; it is not this, but its effect upon herd-instinct, that we are concerned with. The destructiveness of war being greater, the fear of it is greater ; therefore the intensity of national feeling is greater ; and therefore the likelihood of war is greater. It may therefore be laid down as a general proposition that whatever increases the harmfulness of war also increases its likelihood.

II

So far, we have been concerned with the instinct out of which nationalism grows, and with the way in which industrialism increases the stimuli to the operation of this instinct. We have now to pass to a less irrational theme, namely, the way in which industrialism, as it develops, affects the economic relations between nations and the economic motives for national rivalry. It is, of course, obvious that rivalry between nations could not exist unless nations existed, and nations (as we have seen) are a product of instinct. Therefore our analysis of the operation of herd-instinct had to precede the discussion of the economic relations between nations, since it is presupposed in treating nations as economic units.

In the early stages of industry, when an industrial nation contains many competing manufacturers of the same commodity, the connection of each individual firm with the State is very slight. As in the pre-industrial era, a man who makes (say) cotton goods is more conscious of the rivals in his own country who also make cotton goods than he is of the competition of foreigners. This was especially the case in England in the early nineteenth century, when foreign competition hardly existed. Since each man believes himself cleverer than his rivals, each asks nothing of the State except free competition and removal of all restrictions on enterprise. At this stage, it is thought that industry will make for internationalism, since all national barriers are hindrances to commerce. The individual manufacturer is concerned primarily with *selling* his produce. The economic process as a whole consists in the production of goods to satisfy needs. It exists in its integral form when a peasant grows crops to nourish himself and his family, and again, at a later stage, when a State produces goods to be distributed among the citizens according to their needs. But between these two stages lies the com-

mercial epoch, when one man produces and sells to
the merchant, from whom another buys and consumes.
Throughout this epoch, the interest of the producer
in the goods ceases as soon as they are sold ; it is a
matter of indifference to the producer whether they
really satisfy a need, or are only so well advertised that
foolish people (who are sufficiently numerous to make
anybody's fortune) think they will satisfy a need.
Throughout the commercial stage, the chief concern
of the producer is for a market.   The need for markets
has developed a new form of nationalism, arising out
of the combination of commerce with industrial methods
of production.

The stage of national competition for markets
represents the second stage in the relations of industrialism and nationalism.   Before the war, the plant
existing in the industrial nations was sufficient to
produce more of many commodities than could be
sold at a profit.   The stage of many small separate
firms in each country had passed in many industries ;
there were a few large dominant firms, or even only
a single Trust, in each country.   To each of these it
became vitally important to secure a market from which
their rivals were as far as possible excluded.   The
home market (except in the United Kingdom) was
secured by protective tariffs ; the markets of developed
countries were largely closed by the same method.
Hence the struggle became concentrated on the
undeveloped countries, especially in Africa and Asia.
The best way to capture such a market was to induce
one's government to annex the territory concerned.
This led necessarily to conflicts between the governments, supported by their peoples for nationalistic
reasons, under the influence of a vigorous Press
campaign inspired by the firms whose interests were

involved. The natural outcome of this process was the war of 1914–1918—the Great War, as we still call it, though this name will soon cease to be applicable.

The Great War has ushered in a new epoch. Owing to the general destruction, it was for a time more difficult to buy than to sell. The commercial epoch depended upon greater eagerness on the part of the seller than on that of the buyer. During the war, we had experience of the opposite state of affairs. In shopping, it was the purchaser who was grateful when the required article was forthcoming, not the shopkeeper who was glad of the chance to sell. And what applied to small transactions applied also to large ones. This state of affairs was, of course, in part temporary, but it produced everywhere, except in America, some part of the effect which led to Russian Communism. There was a tendency for the State to undertake the purchase or manufacture of neces-, saries, and to distribute them on a system of rationing. This is the economic essence of communism. It is an inevitable result of shortage in supplies, and has always been adopted in sieges and other occasions when the necessaries of life were very scarce. Although the immediate pressure has been relaxed in Western Europe, there are certain broad reasons which make it probable that, in some form or other, the same system must soon reappear.

The third stage in industrial development, which has so far only been completely reached for a short time in Russia, is when a nation is organized as a producing and consuming unit, not primarily as a trader. In this stage trade occurs only for the obtaining of some definitely-needed commodity. Where the government is not actuated by theory (as in Russia) but merely by practical exigencies, this stage will be reached at different times as regards different commodities. The commercial stage will persist as regards goods of which there is a surplus, while the new system will be adopted as regards those of which there is a shortage. Oil is a good example of a commodity of which there is a shortage. Nations which possess oil are not anxious to part with it, whereas those who have none are willing to make great concessions in order to be allowed to become purchasers. As industrialism more and more exhausts the raw materials which it requires, a similar tendency will show itself as regards other things. Coal and iron are already in this category. This stage brings competition among buyers at least equal to that between sellers, and thus destroys the economic superiority of the consumer to the producer, which characterizes the commercial epoch. Competition between nations will increasingly tend to be not for markets, but for raw materials ; that is to say, they will compete as producers, not as traders. It is only with this stage that industrialism becomes fully developed. Its earlier commercial phase is a legacy from the past ; its typical future form is that in which nations are organized as producers, distributing their product among their citizens, as, at an earlier stage, a peasant's family consume the crops which they have jointly produced.

Industrialism in its heyday is being extraordinarily wasteful of the natural resources of the world, taking no thought whatever for future generations. It is probable that, within the lifetime of those who are now young, scarcity of raw materials will radically transform industry, and compel nations to adopt less frantic and excessive methods of production. Some authorities assert that oil, coal, iron and many other hitherto necessary materials of industrialism, will have grown very scarce fifty years hence ; in any case, it is nearly certain that they will have grown sufficiently scarce for those nations which possess them to be anxious to avoid waste. This will be a powerful check to the commercial outlook, which aims at developing all resources feverishly and dumping them upon a reluctant world in a hysterical get-rich-quick campaign. The new industrial outlook will treat a nation's resources as a prudent man treats his capital, not as a spendthrift treats his income. Mines will be worked and land will be cultivated, not, as now, to produce excessive wealth in the present generation, poverty in the next, and starvation in the third, but with a view to providing a continuous livelihood, as well as a continuous defence against armies and navies.

Defence in war is, at present, the most powerful motive driving nations from the commercial to the true industrial outlook. The blockade has been shown to be such a terrible weapon against a trading nation that every great nation now wishes to be self-subsistent as regards the necessaries of life and of war.[1] America is at present completely self-subsistent, though the prospective exhaustion of the oil supplies causes anxiety for the future. The British Empire is self-subsistent so long as command of the seas is retained, but not a day longer. Russia will be self-subsistent as soon as her industry is developed. China could be, given industrial development and a strong army. The tendency of each of these empires will be to aim at minimizing foreign trade, and to confine it to goods which are not indispensable either

---

[1] Hence our interest in empire trade as against foreign trade.

in peace or war.   From sheer self-preservation, every great nation will be compelled to put a stop to the wasteful use of its resources by capitalists who care only for private profit.   The nationalization of raw materials is inevitable as soon as people come to realize how easily they may be exhausted.   Thus in one form or another, national socialism is nearly certain to come in all great States, unless, before that stage is reached, external wars and internal labour conflicts cause the whole industrial machine to break down.   This result is by no means improbable in the present temper of the world ; but if it is not brought about, State owner-ship of raw materials will be an inevitable measure of self-protection on the part of all civilized populations of great States.[1]

Assuming national socialism pretty equally realized among great industrial nations, will it have any effect in diminishing the virulence and destructiveness of nationalism ?   It will, of course, diminish wars for markets, and destroy one of the motives for imperial-ism.   The British have valued India chiefly as a market ; if India belonged to any other Power, British goods would be excluded by a tariff.   This motive for desiring empire would cease.   But another, at least as powerful, would take its place, namely, the desire to own the places which contain valuable raw material. If Great Britain were communist, there would exist the same motive as at present for fighting Russia in Persia and the Caucasus, namely, oil.   It would, in fact, be far easier than it is at present to rouse popular enthusiasm for such a war, since it would then seem obviously in the national interest, whereas now it appears to be only in the interests of a gang of

---

[1] Cf. Salter's *Allied Shipping Control* for examples of the analogous advantages to be obtained from State control of shipping.

capitalists. With the increasing shortage of raw materials, the fight for them will grow keener, and victory will lie with the Power which has the last unexploited resources. This Power will be able to impose its will upon the world, and to live in communistic luxury on the labour of vast populations of slaves. But until that day comes, there seems no reason to expect that national socialism will bring peace to the world, unless the world becomes organized into huge blocks, each strong for defence but unable to attack one of the other blocks successfully.

Socialism is, of course, in theory international, but its internationalism seems to be merely a transitory effect of its world-wide struggle with capitalism. A communist government, as is beginning to appear in Russia, may acquire just as much nationalism as was shown by its capitalistic predecessor. It would be possible, perhaps, for socialism to generate a United States of Europe, which would be undoubtedly a great achievement. It would also be possible, and probably easier, for Russian communism to produce a union of all Asia with the exception of Japan. But it is difficult to imagine socialism producing a union of a European block with Eastern Asia, or of an Asiatic block with Western Europe; and it is still more difficult to imagine a union of either with the United States. It is clear that the tendency to increase in the size of empires must continue, if only for the sake of defence in war. It is clear also that, with the decay of commerce and the development of the submarine, maritime empires are becoming impossible. These considerations suggest the possibility of an organization of the world on some such lines as these: The United States dominating all North and South America; Russia dominating the whole of Asia ; a block of all Europe except Russia dominating the Mediterranean and Africa by closing the Straits of Gibraltar. In such a world, defensive war might be easy and offensive war obviously impossible. The habit of war might then gradually die out, and the relations between different States might become so slight and trivial as to give no grounds for hostility.

Before that stage can be reached, terrible havoc must be wrought by nationalism, unless men can be aroused to a realization that it is a madness. It is to be expected that America will treat Japan as the Allies treated Germany ; that there will then be a great contest between Russia and America for the exploitation of China ; and that Western Europe will have to descend to the very depths of misery before it is led, through the peril of pressure from Russia in the East and America in the West, to forget the ridiculous enmities left by the war. How much will remain of civilization when that day comes is very doubtful. All these disasters can be averted if there comes to be among statesmen any common sense or common humanity, or among peoples any understanding of the fact that in the modern world one can only injure one's enemies by injuring oneself. But the world is in a mood in which hatred outweighs self-interest, and it is possible that men will only grow weary of hatred after the whole cycle of ruin has worked itself out. Patriotism and the class war are the two great dangers to the world in the present age. Material progress has increased men's power of injuring one another, and there has been no correlative moral progress. Until men realize that warfare, which was once a pleasant pastime, has now become race suicide ; until they realize that the indulgence of hatred makes social life impossible with modern powers of destruction, there can be no hope for the world.   It is moral progress that is needed ; men must learn toleration and the avoidance of violence, or civilization must perish in universal degradation and misery.

CHAPTER V

THE TRANSITION
TO INTERNATIONALISM

INDUSTRIALISM, if we have been right in our previous analysis, requires for its harmonious working two things which do not exist at present, namely socialism and internationalism. In the absence of these two, the conflicting passions which it arouses are so fierce, and the means which it puts at our disposal for their gratification are so powerful, that it may be expected within the next hundred years to destroy both itself and our civilization. In that case it will be necessary to begin all over again, as after the barbarian invasion. Possibly that may be in the long run the more desirable alternative. It may be that the débris of our old civilization will require centuries to decay before there is room for anything new to grow up. It may be that civilized life has exhausted men's vigour and initiative, in which case a long period of primitiveness and uninhibited instincts may be required to restore the energy needed for fresh construction. On such matters it would be both rash and useless to have an opinion. Our problem is a more restricted one, namely : If internationalism and socialism are conditions for the prolonged existence of industrialism, what possibility is there of their realization ? What forces leading to their establishment exist or are likely to be generated in the near future ? It is this problem, as regards internationalism, that is to form the subject of the present chapter.

One thing, unfortunately, seems fairly clear. Internationalism will not be brought about, in any near future, by the mere realization that it is desirable, or even that it is imperative for the preservation of everything that we value. At the close of the great war, one might have expected an unusually keen consciousness of the evils of nationalism, and an unusually warm welcome for any proposal tending to minimize the risk of war. Yet the utmost that President Wilson could secure was his League of Nations, a body which rejected Germany and Russia and was rejected by the United States—a body moreover which, in order to safeguard the precious sovereignty of its component nations, can take no decision except unanimously. It is of course obvious at once to everyone that no good, from an international point of view, can be done by any body which does not, in certain respects, limit the sovereignty of separate nations, for it is this unrestricted sovereignty which is the cause of international anarchy. But although this is plain to all, it has very little effect on statesmanship. And in this the statesmen are no worse than the populations they represent.

We have therefore to ask ourselves whether there is any way by which internationalism can come about naturally, without demanding much wisdom on the part of politicians or average citizens.

The internationalism with which we are concerned is not primarily a matter of sentiment, though its possibility or impossibility may in part depend upon sentimental factors. The internationalism with which we are concerned is primarily a matter of world-government, i.e. of the creation or growth of some organization powerful enough to enforce its decisions upon all mankind and therefore able to regulate the relations between nations according to law, not by the relative strengths of the nations in warfare. Such a body would have to deal not only with territorial questions, but with emigration and immigration on any large scale, with the rationing of raw materials, and perhaps ultimately with the distribution of power from international power stations. Imagine, for example, the situation of Switzerland if the European coal supply were exhausted, and for purposes of illustration let us suppose its water power greater than it is. All its powerful neighbours would seek access to Alpine water-power, and, if there were no international government, would find it cheaper, in the end, to annex the Alps than to pay a rent to their inhabitants. Existing arrangements offer no solution of such a problem except exploitation of other countries by the Swiss or subjugation of the Swiss by other countries, either of which would be unjust. Only a strong international government could provide a just solution of the difficulty, or prevent it from becoming an incentive to war.

The reasons for desiring international government are two: first, the prevention of war, secondly, the securing of economic justice as between different nations and different populations. Of these the prevention of war is the more important, both because war (especially as it will become) is more harmful than injustice, and because the grosser forms of injustice will not often be inflicted upon civilized nations except as the result of war. It would not be common, for example, in a time of profound peace to deprive a nation of its means of livelihood and at the same time prevent its population from emigrating, as we have done in Austria. If peace can be preserved, it is probable that some degree of justice will ultimately result. Even if a considerable measure of injustice were to remain, it is probable that the least fortunate populations in a time of secure peace would be better off than the most fortunate in a period of frequent wars. We have therefore to consider internationalism primarily from the point of view of preventing war, and only secondarily from the point of view of justice between nations. This is important because, as we shall see, some of the most probable approaches to international government involve considerable injustice for long periods of time.

The adoption of national socialism by the Great Powers, even if it could be brought about, would not, in the present temper of the world, lead to inter-nationalism. The Australian Labour Party, when it acquired power, showed itself as imperialistic as Mr. Winston Churchill. The Bolsheviks, in their dealings with neighbouring states, have been as imperialistic as they dared. Early in 1922, Trotsky attempted, in the *Daily Herald*, to justify their policy towards Georgia, but his justification was merely that they are no worse than we are, and that the Georgians are stupid. Some of Trotsky's remarks are worth quoting. In the *Daily Herald* for April 1, 1922, he says :—

The Soviet Republic, having inherited the Tsarist Empire, which had been created by violence and oppression, quite openly proclaimed the right of national self-determination and of national independence. Whilst realizing the enormous significance of this watchword during the transition period to Socialism, our party did not for a minute regard it as the dominating factor, in view of the fact that the economic development of present-day society has a strongly centralist character.

Capitalism itself has laid down the preliminary foundations

for a well-regulated economy on a world scale. (Imperialism is only the capitalist expression of the desire to obtain the monopoly of the world's economy.) In the phraseology of the capitalist greed and piracy, the fundamental task of our epoch consists in the establishment of the close relationship between the economic systems of the various parts of the world, and in building up, in the interests of the whole of humanity, co-ordinated world production, based on the most economic use of all forces and means. This is precisely the task of Socialism.

In view of the fact that Trotsky is engaged in justifying an act of aggression (in Georgia) just as bad as any of which capitalist nations have been guilty, one may paraphrase this as proclaiming that what he calls " capitalist greed and piracy " is to be succeeded by proletarian greed and piracy. Why this is an advance he does not explain. He goes on to say (*Daily Herald*, April 3rd) :—

We do not only recognize but we give full support to the principle of self-determination, whenever it is directed against feudal, capitalist and imperialist states. But wherever the fiction of self-determination becomes, in the hands of the bourgeoisie, a weapon directed against the proletarian revolution (as in the case of Georgia), we have no occasion to treat this fiction differently from the other " democratic principles " perverted by Capitalism.

I do not by any means wholly disagree with Trotsky's theoretical attitude in these passages. No nation can be allowed an absolute right of self-determination if a world-government is to be created ; and without a world-government it will be impossible to preserve civilization for another hundred years. But I cannot admit the right of a single nation, whether the British, the Americans, or the Russians, to claim for themselves rights which belong essentially to an as yet non-existent international authority. Georgia contains oil ;· therefore the Russians conflicted with the British and the French for possession of the oil. It is contrary to all sound socialist doctrine that the oil should be the private property of Georgia, but there is no better reason why it should belong to Soviet Russia. It ought to belong to a world-wide combination, which would ration it to the various countries according to their needs and their economic suitability for using it. Cases like the Suez and Panama Canals are analogous. It would be absurd for them to belong absolutely to the people who live near them ; but that is no reason why they should belong to England and the United States respectively. If England and the United States were socialistic, they would have no better right to the canals than they have now, but might be just as anxious to retain them as Trotsky is to retain the Georgian oil. National socialism therefore will not solve our problem.

Far the easiest road to international government would be the unquestionable preponderance of some one State. That State would then be so strong that no other would venture to quarrel with it, and it might for its own purposes forbid the others to fight among themselves, as we, for example, have prevented Esthonia, Latvia and Lithuania from exterminating each other since self-determination set them nominally free to do so. What makes this road so easy is that it requires no voluntary restraint of the instincts of nationalism and domination which are developed by the existing forms of industrialism, and that it can therefore be brought about without any fundamental change of policy on the part of anyone.

The only question—but by no means a small one—is, whether any State is strong enough to acquire such a unique position. Spain, France and Germany made the attempt and were defeated—Spain by the resistance of England, France and Holland ; France by the resistance of England, Germany and Russia ; Germany by the resistance of England, France and America. England has hitherto always been a decisive factor in preserving that state of anarchy which our grandfathers called " The liberties of Europe " ; and our success has been the source of our power. But shall we preserve this good fortune ? Shall we be equally successful in resisting the next bid for world-empire ? As a patriot I fear, and as an internationalist I hope, that this is doubtful.

It is of course obvious that the next Power to make a bid for world empire will be America. America may not, as yet, consciously desire such a position, but no nation with sufficient resources can long resist the attempt. And the resources of America are more adequate than those of any previous aspirant to universal hegemony. First of all, America is self-supporting in all the necessaries of peace and war ; both industry and agriculture could be preserved in almost complete efficiency without commerce with any other continent. Secondly, America has the largest white population of any State except Russia, and its population is superlatively skilled, energetic and physically courageous. Thirdly, Canada would have to side with America in any serious war, if only for reasons of self-preservation ; and Mexico would be unable to refuse access to its mineral resources. Therefore the whole of North America must be counted as belonging to the United States in considering the possibilities of a world war. Fourthly, America could, after the outbreak of war, build a sufficiently powerful navy to defeat any possible hostile naval combination. Fifthly, all Europe is in America's debt, and we in England are dependent on America for our very existence, owing to our need of raw cotton and Canadian wheat. Lastly, the Americans surpass even the British in sagacity, apparent moderation, and the skilful use of a hypocrisy by which even they themselves are deceived. Against such a combination of resources no existing State could hope to prove victorious.

These facts are perhaps not obvious to all statesmen ; they were not obvious to the Germans during the war, and are not now fully recognized in Japan. But it would seem that both England and America are quite aware of their significance. Our statesmen understand that friendship with America is necessary to our continued existence as a Great Power. They know that our naval and industrial supremacy, which gave us the victory in previous wars, would no longer exist in a war with America, and that if we were to fight America, even in alliance with Japan, the end would be our complete collapse. It must therefore be our policy to preserve the friendship of America if possible, at no matter what cost to ourselves. Nor is this to be regretted for the present, since the international policy of the United States, except as regards Russia, is, as yet, more liberal and less imperialistic than our own. This is particularly the case in China, where we, while our alliance with Japan lasted, at least passively supported Japanese aggression, and threw the bulk of our influence against attempts to introduce a liberal and stable government. For the moment, therefore, the influence of America in world politics must be regarded as fortunate, since the ambitions of America are commercial rather than territorial.

The influence of America in the world is bound up with that of high finance. I fear I shall incur the displeasure of most socialists if I say that high finance seems to me, at this moment, in certain respects, the sanest and most constructive influence in the western world. Believing, as I do, that the goal is international socialism, I believe also that, at this moment, internationalism is more important than socialism. Although socialists profess internationalism, they do not seem to me, at present, to be able to be practical internationalists. In these days of unemployment, for example, the fear of German competition would make it very difficult for a Labour Government to adopt unrestricted free trade with Germany. And it will certainly be a long time before socialists are in a position to create the machinery of international government. High finance, on the other hand, is ready to do so, and is impelled in that direction by urgent motives of self-interest. It is easy to imagine, a few years hence, a combination of Morgans in America, the banking interests in this country, Stinnes in Germany, and leading Bolsheviks in Russia, joining together in an informal committee to dominate the policies of their respective governments.[1] For the present, the Bolsheviks cannot easily be admitted, because they refuse to subscribe to the dogma that private property is sacred, upon which all high finance pretends to rest. But Russia's need of foreign credits is compelling the Bolsheviks to a nominal admission of the Russian debt, and as everyone knows that Russia cannot actually pay, a nominal admission may be enough to placate the financiers. Thus Russia may become a

---

[1] See a very interesting memorandum prepared on behalf of the Industrial Group in the House of Commons (*The Times*, March 8, 1923), which says (*inter alia*): "An economic alliance between this country, Russia, Germany, and the United States would be impossible to resist, even by the foremost military Power of Europe." It proceeds to give reasons for regarding such an alliance as desirable and practicable, and to discuss the opposition to be expected from France.

party to the policy of the Washington and Genoa Conferences. This policy has two sides. From the point of view of the financiers, it is an attempt to prevent what they have lent to the belligerents from becoming a bad debt, and to find in Europe and Asia fields for the investment of fresh capital. From the point of view of Germany, Russia and China, it is an attempt to revive or create industry so as to become solvent and ultimately rich and powerful. For the moment, the interests of the two sides are more or less in agreement. It is therefore conceivable that an international government might grow up in this way. But though conceivable, I do not think it is probable, for reasons which I will briefly set forth.

There is, first of all, a powerful opposition from the point of view of a narrow nationalism. France and Japan think that they can acquire more wealth by means of their armies than by means of finance ; therefore they oppose everything that would tend to make peace secure. France is supported, for nationalist reasons, by Poland, Czecho-Slovakia, Rumania, Serbia and Turkey, and we dare not be very hostile to Turkey because of the Indian Mohammedans. Therefore France and Japan cannot be simply brushed aside so long as Germany and Russia remain weak, but Germany and Russia cannot be restored at all quickly while France and Japan remain powerful and hostile to them. High finance does not want another great war at present, since that would mean the bankruptcy of its debtors. High finance, relying upon its dogma of the sacredness of private property, has not yet quite understood that, in all international dealings, the security of a loan rests ultimately upon armies and navies. To speak more exactly : when an American citizen lends money to a European or Asiatic Government he must be in a position to threaten that government with disaster in the event of repudiation. For this purpose, he must be able, should necessity arise, to induce his own government to act energetically, and his own government must be able to inflict grievous injury upon the defaulting foreign government. This requires a general policy of imperialism, which the American people have hitherto shown themselves reluctant to adopt. To meet this difficulty, the financiers appeal to the lofty standards of American morality. Most nations likely to default fall short, in some respect, of the New England standard. The Chinese are heathen, and some of them are polygamous. The Russians practise free love. The British are guilty of atrocities in Ireland and India. The Germans are the Germans. It is therefore possible to get up a moral crusade whenever it may be necessary. This was done successfully when America came into the war in 1917, but it cannot be done very often, as each time a certain number of people afterwards see through the trick. The limits of human gullibility are among the limits of the powers of high finance.

But even supposing the creditor nations could be induced to support their financiers, and the nationalist policy of France and Japan could be overcome, there would infallibly be friction between lending and borrowing nations as soon as the latter were in any degree restored to a normal economic life. For the moment, Germany and Russia may be forced to accept almost any terms ; but the financiers must, in their own interests, restore the industries of these countries, which will reassert their independence as soon as they feel strong enough to do so. Experience has shown that the Bolsheviks were premature in repudiating the Russian debt ; but the time for such an action will come. And if it were adopted simultaneously by all debtor nations, it is not likely that the power of international finance over those nations could be restored. I do not think, therefore, that international government will be realized in any near future through the method of the Consortium.

There is, however, another possibility, to which we must now turn our attention, namely, that of great land empires, strong for defence but weak for attack. But before considering this possibility, we must say a few words as to the relations of England and America.

It would be exceedingly rash to hazard a prophecy as to the future of Anglo-American relations. Nevertheless it seems as if one of two things must happen, either an alliance in which the British Empire would take second place, or a war in which the British Empire would be dissolved. An alliance would only be possible if we sincerely abandoned all furtherance of our own imperialism and all opposition to that of America. If this should happen, an English-speaking block could very largely control the world, and make first-class wars improbable during its existence. Possibly the result would not be very different if there were a struggle for supremacy between England and America, ending in the defeat of England. The Dominions would in that case gravitate to America, and the only difference would be that the United Kingdom would belong to the European system instead of to the English-speaking group. Fortunately, all present indications, especially since the settlement of the debt question, point to growing friendship between ourselves and the United States, which is the only sane policy for us, and will, I hope, continue to be favoured by the Americans.

The essential point in these speculations is that the day for great maritime and commercial empires appears to be passing. It seems probable that great empires, in future, will have to be based upon vast tracts of land, producing all that is indispensable for the existence of their population, and not absolutely dependent upon external trade for their subsistence. This is due partly to the potency of the blockade as a weapon against a commercial nation, and partly to the increasing difficulty of safeguarding maritime communications in time of war against submarines and aeroplanes. But there is also another reason, reinforced by these, though not wholly derived from them, and that is, the increasing desire of every great State to be self-subsistent and not vitally dependent upon foreigners. Before we arrive at any form of internationalism, it is probable that we shall pass through a phase of large empires, each more or less closed against all the others, each therefore able to defend itself though not able to attack any other large empire successfully.

This likelihood is reinforced by a consideration of the limits to which American power would be subject if it were developed to its fullest extent. There are at present two land empires comparable to America in potential strength, namely, Russia and China. Western Europe, if it were united, might form a third, and could be economically self-subsistent if it retained Africa. Against such empires, if their military and industrial resources were developed, no other Power or combination of Powers could prevail; they would have the same kind of invulnerability that America already has. Russia has been taught a bitter lesson in the dangers of dependence upon foreign countries, and will free itself if freedom is possible. China is only beginning to learn the lesson, but is likely to have mastered it thoroughly before another hundred years have passed.

The world at present is in a state of confusion and instability produced by the artificial provisions of the Versailles Treaty and by the childish application of the principle of self-determination in Eastern Europe. Instability is the enemy of peace; any arrangement which could easily be upset by a war is an incitement to militarism. The small nations of Europe, which exist only so long as England and France are willing and able to give them military protection, will have to forgo their petty prides and absurd hatreds. It is monstrous that Czecho-Slovakia or Jugo-Slavia should be free to refuse to trade with Austria or Hungary, and that the Baltic States should be able to block intercourse between Germany and Russia. Such rights can, unfortunately, be exacted by the strong; but that they should be voluntarily conceded to the weak is an example of Wilsonian liberalism run mad. The small States of Europe will have to be forced, if necessary, to concede free trade and freedom of intercourse between each other and between neighbouring Great Powers. Gradually, if Europe is to survive, it will have to develop a central government controlling its international relations. If it cannot do this, it will become, and will deserve to become, the slave of the United States.

For those who only know Europe and European history, it is difficult to realize the unimportance of the various little bits of nations into which Europe is divided. The time when the history of the world was made in Europe is past. America and Russia are the great independent Powers of the present day. Japan and Great Britain, being dependent upon sea

power, cannot hope to retain their present position ;
on the other hand China may at any moment embark
upon a career which would make it the equal of
Russia. China, with its present weakness and potential strength, is the centre of world politics. The
contest at the moment is between America and Japan,
with England, until the Washington Conference,
half-heartedly on the side of Japan ; Russia, and
China itself, count for nothing in this contest. But
the ultimate form of the conflict is likely to be very
different. In the near future, the situation will
presumably be dominated by the agreement which
has been reached for the three Powers to exploit
China jointly by a Consortium, but ultimately it is
by no means unlikely that there will be war between
Japan and the United States, giving America all that
Japan has hitherto held as well as a consolidation of
the American position in Canton. In spite of the
agreement which has been reached, the imperialisms
of the three Powers involved must bring a conflict
sooner or later, and a conflict must bring victory to
America. Thus of the three present disputants
America is almost certain to be the sole victor in
the end.

The Chinese, at present, abhor the Japanese, dislike
the English, and love the Americans. But the notion
that one great nation is either more virtuous or less
virtuous than another does not survive experience,
and ultimately Chinese hatred will be directed im-
partially against whatever nations have power to
exploit China. It would be easy for the Chinese
to form secret societies, and on a given day assassinate
every foreigner in China. If such an action were
preceded by an alliance with Russia and a certain
amount of secret military preparation (which would

always be possible in western provinces), it would
probably succeed in putting an end for ever to
American influence in China. There is no difficulty
in imagining British rule in India dealt with after the
same fashion. We cannot hope to keep on bringing
civilization to the poor benighted Asiatics without
their ultimately learning its spirit and methods.
Japan has already done so ; China and India may be
expected to follow Japan's example. When that
happens, it will become impossible for Europeans or
Americans or Japanese to retain any power on the
mainland of Asia. It is quite possible, however, that
the Russians, who are really Asiatic and have shown
amazing powers of assimilation in Persia, Mongolia
and Afghanistan, will be able to establish a firm
alliance with India and China, in which case the whole
of Asia and European Russia will become, from an
international point of view, a single invulnerable
block.

What, meanwhile, will become of Europe ? There
would seem to be two main possibilities, one the
partition of Europe between Russia and America,
the other the formation of a United States of Europe.
A partition is not, of course, to be conceived as a
formal annexation : England, France, Germany and
Italy would retain legal and nominal independence,
just as Poland and Jugo-Slavia and Czecho-Slovakia
do at present. But in fact each of these powers
would be in economic alliance either with the west
or with the east ; and being unable to supply all their
own needs, their diplomacy would have to be subservient to one or other of their two great neighbours.
If Russia had been well supplied with food ready for
export, and had had an army capable of completely
defeating the Poles, it is probable that Germany

would have become allied with Russia before now. The effective frontier between Russia and America might be at the Straits of Dover, or the Rhine, or the eastern frontier of Poland. However that may be, the effective independence of Europe cannot possibly be preserved if its little nations (the so-called Great Powers) preserve their divisions and hatreds and quarrels in the presence of their more powerful neighbours. The situation is analogous to that of ancient Greece in face of Macedonia, or of renaissance Italy in face of France and Spain. If division is to continue no ultimate issue is possible except subjugation. The only question, in each case, will be whether the overlord is to be Russia or the United States.

It is, however, just possible that the European nations may in time come to consider their own happiness more desirable than each other's unhappiness. In that case, they may co-operate to restore order in Europe, to rebuild what they have destroyed, and to force the puppet States of the Treaty of Versailles to live in friendly economic relations with each other. There are two ways in which this may be brought about. One is the union of all Europe west of Russia (including Great Britain). Such a union would be strong enough to stand even against such huge aggregations as America and Asia. But there would be some conditions which would have to be fulfilled. It would be necessary to be able to protect our communications with France in time of war, by closing the Straits of Dover by nets (as was done in the late war), by Channel Tunnels, by aeroplanes, or by whatever means science might have made available. It would also be necessary to retain Africa, since no group of nations can be economically self-subsistent without free access to tropical products. This would require the preservation of the Mediterranean as a European lake. It would be easy to close the western entrance against America, but rather more difficult to close the eastern entrance against Russia, since this would require control of the Dardanelles and Bosphorus, and therefore secure possession of Constantinople. Seeing, however, that this would be the only serious military task to be faced by a league of West European nations, it is probable that it could be achieved. In that case, Western Europe could become economically self-subsistent, and strong enough in a military sense to resist any probable aggression without much difficulty.

There is however another possibility, which is much more to the fore at the present time. France is seeking to re-establish the Franco-Russian Alliance, and is hoping to force Germany into complete subservience. The present goal of French policy seems to be an alliance, or understanding, between all the nations of the Continent, including Russia, to be motived mainly by hostility to ourselves. Germany and Russia have no direct motive for preferring France to Great Britain, but France is better able to injure them, and has therefore the first claim to be placated. The policy is difficult of fulfilment, but perhaps not impossible. It has been set forth by the Paris correspondent of *The Times* in a series of telegrams dated February 21, 23, 25 and 26, 1923, more or less corroborated by a leading article in *The Times* of February 26th. The telegrams set forth the difficulties of the policy, as well as the indications that it is being attempted. The two doubtful factors in Europe are Great Britain and Russia. Great Britain may become more and more associated with America and the Dominions, and less and less concerned with the

Continent. Russia may seek hegemony in Asia, as has been happening since the Bolsheviks were sent to Coventry, or may re-enter the sphere of European politics. The French policy adumbrated in *The Times* assumes that Russia will be in the European system and Great Britain outside it. The other policy, which we considerd first, would include Great Britain in Europe and make Russia essentially an Asiatic Power. Both alike would produce a great European block, but the French policy would destroy our influence on the Continent and greatly diminish Russia's influence in Asia.

An organization of the world on some such lines as we have been suggesting is possible by the mere operation of the old forces—greed and fear and self-defence. There is therefore no reason to regard it as a Utopian impossibility. Nevertheless, if it came about, it would have all the advantages of the most idealistic schemes of ardent internationalists. War will only cease when it no longer presents hopes of gain to short-sighted and bloodthirsty nations. This is only possible when every State is strong for defence and weak for attack. The British Empire at present is strong for attack and weak for defence ; our strength for attack prompts our own imperialism, while our weakness for defence affords a constant temptation to the nascent imperialism of America. China is weak both for attack and defence. These two are the main sources of danger to the world's peace in the near future. A State can only be strong for defence when it contains within itself all that is necessary for both peace and war, and when the communications between its different parts cannot easily be interrupted. This points to vast land empires as the States of the future ; and of such States America and Russia are at present the only examples. China could be a third, given good government ; but of that there is no immediate prospect. It is therefore not improbable that China will ultimately come under the hegemony of Russia. If that were to happen, and if Western Europe were either united into one firm alliance or partitioned between America and Russia, offensive war would be everywhere obviously hopeless, and defensive war obviously easy. Under such circumstances, it is very unlikely that wars would occur.

If the whole world were organized into a few great States, each economically self-subsistent and having only trivial commercial relations with other States, economic causes of conflict would be practically eliminated. The impossibility of achieving anything notable by war would make men gradually forget the possibility of fighting, and arrangements for mutual disarmament would become easy. States would then only keep such armies as were necessary for internal order, particularly for the suppression of insurgent nationalities within their own borders. Subordinate nationalities should be allowed autonomy, but not control over foreign policy or over raw materials or over freedom of trade and communication within the State. Claims for control over these matters on the part of component nations within the State should be treated just as severely as claims for liberty to commit murder on the part of an individual. In time the reasonableness of these arrangements would become obvious to all, and even internal armies would cease to be necessary.

The claim to complete national independence on the part of every group which happens to have the sentiment of nationality is quite incompatible with the continued existence of an ordered society. It is only by means of very large States that war can be gradually eliminated, and where large States exist they ought not, in general, to be disrupted because some of their inhabitants wish to be free to kill others without breaking the law. All the legitimate claims of small nationalities can be met by local autonomy ; to grant more is to give way to anarchy. The rights of a nation as against humanity are no more absolute than the rights of an individual as against the community. In the middle ages the barons contended for the right of private war ; nowadays small nations set up the same claim. It is regrettable that big nations should claim such a right, but there is no force capable of restraining them, whereas small nations can be restrained and therefore should be. In time, by the consequent growth of large States and diminution in the importance of economic international relations, the causes of war may be removed. When that has been achieved, men's habits of thought will gradually change in such a way as to make true international government for the whole world possible. But it is useless to hope that this can be achieved while the danger of war is still a daily and pressing menace.

CHAPTER VI

SOCIALISM IN UNDEVELOPED COUNTRIES

IN the last chapter we found a possibility, though by no means a certainty, that what is in effect internationalism may come about during the present century by the growth of vast land empires containing most of the population and resources of the world. If this happens, wars between different States will no longer be a menace to the continued existence of industrial civilization. We have now to consider a more difficult question, namely, the class war and the transition to socialism.

What do we mean by "socialism"? The word is often used very vaguely, but it is not difficult to give it a precise meaning. The definition of socialism consists of two parts, one economic and one political, one concerned with the production and distribution of goods, the other with the distribution of power.

As regards production, all land and capital must be the property of the State—though perhaps the State might sometimes delegate possession to some large body of producers or consumers, such as a trade union or a co-operative society. As regards distribution, what is paid for each kind of work must be fixed by a public authority, with a minimum of what is required for bare necessaries, and a maximum of what will give the greatest incentive to efficient work.

There is no need of equality of income for all as part of the definition of socialism ; the fact that Chaliapin is paid more than a scene-shifter does not suffice to prove that Russia is still bourgeois. What is essential is that a man should not be able to extort profit by his possession of means of production, whether land or capital. But socialism certainly has as its ideal equality of income, subject only to such modification as may be imposed by the special needs of various classes of workers.

On the political side, socialism is not compatible with autocracy or oligarchy, but demands that all sane adults should have an equal share of ultimate political power. Even the Bolsheviks, who oppose democracy during the time of transition, regard it as part of their ideal, and admit that socialism will not be fully realized until it is possible to restore liberal democratic institutions, such as universal suffrage, free speech and free press. (This appears in their writings, and was confirmed by Kamenev in a conversation I had with him while in Russia.) The different forms of socialism—State socialism, guild socialism, etc.—do not differ on this point, but only on the extent to which proximate political power is concentrated in the democratic State or diffused through various federated bodies.

For reasons which we have already considered it seems impossible that industrialism should continue efficient much longer unless it becomes socialistic. This is partly because the system of private profit rouses the discontent of the workers and gives them a sense of injustice, partly because the private ownership of land and capital confers upon the owners a degree of control both over private citizens and over the State which is dangerous, since it is used to increase private power and profit and not for the benefit of the community. But the transition from the present system to socialism is full of difficulty, and it is doubtful whether the attempt will succeed or will result in a return to barbarism.

Marx, whose prophetic insight was remarkable but not impeccable, conceived the transition with a schematic simplicity which does not appear at all likely to be realized. He thought—as was natural from the experience of England in the first half of the nineteenth century—that the line between capitalist and proletarian would always remain quite sharp so long as capitalism survived, and that the proletarian could never obtain more than starvation wages, i.e. just enough to keep himself and his family alive. Gradually the capitalists would grow fewer through the concentration of capital, and the proletariat would grow more discontented and more organized through experience of their misfortunes and struggles against them. Their struggles would be first local, then national, then international; when they became international they would be victorious, owing to the immense numerical preponderance of the proletariat. Then, suddenly, by a revolution, the whole economic system would be changed, and international socialism would be established.

In all these respects Marx has proved to be partly mistaken. The line between capitalist and proletarian is not sharp: trade union leaders with comfortable incomes enjoy bourgeois comfort, associate with capitalists on equal terms, and often acquire much of the capitalist mentality. The iron law of wages, invented by orthodox economists to discourage trade unions, and accepted by Marx to encourage revolution, was an economic fallacy: wages in

America, and even in England, now afford far more than a bare subsistence to the majority of wage-earners. The concentration of capital in few large enterprises has not meant a diminution in the number of capitalists, owing to the growth of joint-stock companies. The proletariat have not grown more discontented ; they were certainly more revolutionary in England a hundred years ago than they are now. It is true that they have grown more organized nationally, but the war showed the complete futility, up to the present, of international organization. And if to-morrow a war were to break out between America and Japan, the proletariat of both countries would equal the capitalists in enthusiasm and surpass them in patriotism. Finally, the numerical preponderance of the proletariat has only been realized in a very few countries (of which Great Britain is one). Elsewhere they are outnumbered by the peasant proprietors, who as a rule side with the capitalists. In this last respect, however, time may yet justify Marx. Lenin's scheme of electrification is designed to industrialize agriculture, and thus give to the peasant the mentality of the proletarian. It is possible that technical improvement in agricultural methods may produce a similar change, less intentionally, in other countries. This is a very important consideration, and one which may decide the whole future of socialism, but unfortunately it is a matter as to which prophecy is exceedingly difficult.

The establishment of a communist government in Russia brought to the fore a new set of considerations, which partly confirm and partly confute Marx. The Bolsheviks attempted to establish communism in a country almost untouched by capitalistic industrialism. This raises the question whether capitalism is, as

Marx believed, a necessary stage on the road to socialism, or whether industry can be developed socialistically from the outset in a hitherto undeveloped country. For the future of Russia and Asia this question is of the most vital importance.

The Bolsheviks came into power with the intention of establishing communism at the earliest possible moment, and this intention they no doubt still entertain. But apart from all external difficulties, the internal obstacles have proved greater than they expected. This led them to adopt what is called the "New Economic Policy," which is, at any rate for the moment, a practical abandonment of communism. The reasons for this step may be gathered from a very candid article on "The Meaning of the Agricultural Tax" by Lenin, published in English in the first number of *The Labour Monthly* (July 1921).[1] What he says of Russia would be equally applicable to a socialistic China, or to India if it threw off the British yoke and became Bolshevik. Lenin distinguishes, in present-day Russia, elements at five different levels of economic development, namely :

1. Patriarchal, i.e. to a large degree primitive, peasant production.
2. Small commodity production. (This includes the majority of peasants who sell corn.)
3. Private Capitalism.
4. State Capitalism.
5. Socialism.

The term "State Capitalism" occurs frequently in this article, as well as in others of his writings. It seems to mean the running of enterprises by the State for profit, i.e. in the same way as they would be run by private capitalists. It appears in the course of

[1] See also Lenin's speech on "The New Economic Policy and the Tasks of Political Enlightenment," December 1921.

the article that it includes the running of railways by the State, whether in Soviet Russia or in pre-war Germany. The term is not defined in the article, and I do not profess to know its exact meaning. But the essence of the matter seems to be that under State Capitalism the State *sells* the goods or services concerned, instead of supplying them gratis to those who have a claim to them.

Lenin regards the later stages as higher in the economic scale than the earlier ones, and considers any development from one of them to the next as an advance. He also *seems* to hold—though this is scarcely reconcilable with Bolshevik policy—that no stage can be skipped, but all must be passed through in their proper order. He argues that small commodity production must be encouraged because it is an advance on patriarchal peasant production; that large-scale private capitalism is better than small production (though he hardly ventures to say his government should encourage it); that State capitalism should not be opposed by socialists, because it is so much better than private capitalism; and that socialism cannot be brought about quickly even by a government which bends its whole energies to this task. He quotes the following passage from a pamphlet of his written in 1918:

. . . State Capitalism would be a step in advance in the present state of affairs of our Soviet Republic. If, for example, State Capitalism could establish itself here during the next six months, it would be an excellent thing and a sure guarantee that within a year Socialism will have established itself and become invincible.

Later on in the article he says:

In the above-quoted arguments of 1918, there are a number of errors in connection with periods. Periods prove to be much longer than was then assumed.

But the question of speed need not concern us at present ; it is the nature and direction of the movement towards socialism in undeveloped countries that I wish to investigate.

If one examines Lenin's argument closely, one finds (if I am not mistaken) that its upshot is this : A government of convinced communists can limit the phase of private capitalism to rather small businesses, replacing large-scale private capitalism by State capitalism ; also they can, by propaganda and by initiating industrial advances, enormously accelerate the movement from any one phase to the next ; but they cannot enable a community to skip any of the phases altogether, or overcome the laws of economic evolution.

A few further quotations will help to elucidate the position taken up in this very important pronouncement.

State Capitalism is incomparably higher *economically* than our present economic system (i.e. that of Russia in 1921).

Socialism is impossible without large capitalist technique.

Socialism is impossible without the domination of the proletariat in the State.

I will, first of all, quote a concrete example of State Capitalism. Everybody will know this example : Germany.

A victorious proletarian revolution in Germany would immediately and with tremendous ease smash the whole shell of imperialism . . . and would for certain bring about the victory of world Socialism.

If the revolution in Germany is delayed our task becomes clear, to learn State Capitalism from the Germans, and to exert all our efforts to acquire it. We must not spare any dictatorial methods in hastening the Westernization of barbarous Russia, and stick at no barbarous methods to combat barbarism.

The problem of power is the root problem of all revolutions.

Our poverty and ruin is such that we cannot *immediately* establish large State Socialist Factory Production.

It is necessary to a certain extent to assist the re-establishment of *small industry*, which does not require machinery.

What is the result of all this ? Fundamentally, we get a certain amount (if only local) of Free Trade, a revival of the petty bourgeoisie and Capitalism. This is undoubted, and to close one's eyes to it would be ridiculous.

After explaining the folly of attempting to prevent all private trading, with a half-confession of the fact that this policy has been vigorously pursued hitherto, he explains the new policy which he now advocates :

Or (and this is the only *possible* and sensible policy) we can refrain from prohibiting and preventing the development of Capitalism and strive to direct it in the path of *State* Capitalism. This is economically possible, for State Capitalism exists in one or another form and to one or another extent everywhere where there are elements of Free Trade and Capitalism in general.

He proceeds to mention concessions and co-operative societies as examples of this policy.

On the subject of fitting the peasantry into a socialist system, he says :

Is it possible to realize the direct transition of this state of pre-capitalist relations prevailing in Russia to Socialism ? Yes, it is possible to a certain degree, but only on one condition, which we know, thanks to the completion of a tremendous scientific labour. That condition is : electrification. But we know very well that this " one " condition demands at least ten years of work, and we can only reduce this period by a victory of the proletarian revolution in such countries as England, Germany, and America.

Capitalism is an evil in comparison with Socialism, but Capitalism is a blessing in comparison with mediævalism.

It must be the aim of all true workers to get local industry thoroughly going in the country districts, hamlets and villages, no matter on how small a scale. The economic policy of the State must concentrate on this. Any development in local industry is a firm foundation, and a sure step, in the building-up of large-scale industry.

I have thought it necessary to make these numerous quotations, because they contain admissions, based on experience, of many things which socialistic critics have vainly urged upon the Bolsheviks both in Europe and Asia. The problem of what can and what cannot be done towards the hastening of the advent of Socialism in undeveloped or partially-developed countries, is made much clearer by Lenin's exposition of his difficulties. The great importance of the problem lies in the fact that, while technical and economic conditions are more favourable to socialism in advanced countries, the political conditions are more favourable in backward countries, for reasons which I shall discuss presently. If, therefore, the technical difficulties could be overcome by the Bolsheviks, they would have immensely facilitated the introduction of world-Socialism. But the Bolshevik method has not only the difficulties recognized by Lenin. It has also others at least as formidable, as I shall now try to show. The result seems to be that, in spite of the political difficulties, there is more hope of the inauguration of successful socialism in the advanced countries than in those which have hitherto escaped any large development of capitalistic industrialism.

Industrialism in an undeveloped country (as we saw in an earlier chapter) must be aristocratic, and must at first entail great poverty for the bulk of the population unless it is inaugurated by foreign capital. The Bolsheviks are obliged to manage industry as autocratically as any Trust magnate, and are unable to afford more than a bare subsistence to their employees. Moreover, the attempt to dispense with the assistance of foreign capitalists has had to be abandoned since the resumption of trade and the adoption of the policy of concessions. The policy of developing industrialism without outside help entails such terrible hardships, over and above those that are in any case inevitable, that no nation, not even Soviet Russia, can face them. It is true that in England industrialism was built up without foreign capital, but the circumstances were very special, and not such as can be repeated. Coal and iron were plentiful and in close proximity to each other ; new inventions, all English and confined to England by the Napoleonic wars, were cheapening production enormously ; and above all, there were no other industrial nations to compete. In spite of all these advantages, the poverty and overwork of the operatives were appalling, and such as can only be imposed upon a nation subject to an aristocratic tyranny. We cannot hope, therefore, that a modern undeveloped nation, without special advantages, can become industrial without the help of foreign capital.

Under these circumstances, is it possible for a country like Russia or China to pass straight to what Lenin calls State Capitalism, without passing through the stage of large-scale private capitalism ? To make the matter concrete, is it possible to have railways, docks, etc., built and owned by the State, and mines worked by the State, by means, partly, of borrowed capital, but without allowing the lenders any voice in the management ? A strong State can do analogous things for ordinary purposes ; for example, the holders of war loan were not allowed a representative at G.H.Q. to see that the war yielded good dividends. Nor did the French investors who lent to the Tsarist government demand a voice in the management of the secret police, although they knew that revolution might mean repudiation. In such matters, it is assumed that the interests of governments and their creditors are identical, and that therefore governments need not be interfered with by private capitalists. But in the development of new industrial resources a different point of view is customary, and a government can seldom effect a loan without selling some part of the national independence. In China, for example, foreign investors expect the concession of monopoly rights—customs, railways, mines, etc.— before they will lend to a government. This makes State capitalism impossible in so far as the rights granted to foreigners are concerned. The money that they lend to the government is spent in bribery, paying troops, etc., not in productive enterprises ; the productive enterprises remain in the hands of foreign capitalists.

In Russia, the Bolsheviks hope to restrain this policy of concessions within narrow limits, and to retain the bulk of the nation's resources in the hands of the State. If they could succeed decisively, the Russian State, or perhaps the communist party, might in the end replace the foreign capitalist as the exploiter of China, and might acquire a hold there which foreign nations would find very hard to loosen. The success or failure of Russia will probably decide whether it is possible to pass to Socialism through State Capitalism rather than through large-scale private capitalism. If the Bolsheviks succeed, Asia may escape the advanced forms of private capitalism ; if they fail, the whole world will probably have to arrive at the stage at which the advanced industrial countries are now.

The success or failure of the Bolsheviks turns on three kinds of factors, military, economic, and moral.

It is, of course, obvious that success is impossible without an army sufficiently strong to repel all attacks that can be easily provoked. Any trade agreements the Bolsheviks conclude are the fruit of their success in defeating Koltchak and Denikin and holding the Poles at bay. If at any moment a combination of (say) Japanese, Poles and Rumanians had a good chance of defeating them, such a combination would, of course, at once declare a holy war against them. The only thing that may in time alter this state of feeling will be the investment of large amounts of new foreign capital in the form of concessions which a White government might repudiate. It is chiefly the military strength of Russia that gives it pre-eminence above other undeveloped countries.

The economic factors introduce more difficult considerations. It is necessary for the Bolsheviks first to import from abroad the minimum of machinery, rolling-stock, etc., required for reviving agriculture and restoring industry to its pre-war level. When this has been done, and it has become possible to purchase food from the peasants by supplying them with goods instead of paper, it will become possible to revive and increase the pre-war export of food and raw materials, and at the same time to develop Russian industry enormously. It is the early steps in this process that are the most difficult and dangerous. Imports are needed first of all, and although a few of the most indispensable can be paid for in gold, the bulk will have to be paid for in concessions, since exports are impossible in these days of famine and collapse of transport. Russia's need being desperate, the concession-hunters will exact very severe terms. Each concession will become a centre of private trading, and will make it more difficult to keep the bulk of foreign commerce in the hands of the State. There will be loopholes for corruption, and it may well be doubted how much of the later phases in the economic recovery will take place on the lines of State capitalism. All these difficulties are in no way peculiar to Russia, but are bound to occur in any undeveloped country which attempts a method of development disliked by foreign capitalists. But though the difficulties are great, they are not economically insuperable ; by sufficient honesty, determination, and energy on the part of the rulers they could probably all be overcome in time.

This brings us to the moral factors of success. It is here that the difficulties of the Bolshevik programme are greatest. Few governments in history have had more honesty, determination, and energy than the Soviet government ; yet it may well be doubted whether even they, in the end, will be found to have enough for the carrying-out of their original intentions. If the periods of time involved had been, as Lenin believed in 1918, six months or a year, or even a few years, the men who initiated the movement could have themselves carried it to a triumphant conclusion without any great change meanwhile in their own outlook and disposition. But it is now six years since the October revolution, and by Lenin's confession the work is scarcely begun. When the Bolsheviks speak of the period during which the dictatorship will have to continue, they seem to contemplate at least a generation. Meanwhile many of the original leaders will have died, while those who remain and those who replace them will have acquired the habit of arbitrary power. The practice of negotiating with capitalists and their governments will tend to produce an acceptance of their assumptions, as it often does in trade union leaders. Capitalists will endeavour to extend their concessions, and will offer corrupt bargains to induce such extensions. It is hardly to be assumed that all officials will be always incorruptible.

It is, of course, possible, for a time, to secure a very high moral level through enthusiasm and hope. Revolutionary ardour will do wonders while it lasts, but it does not last for ever. The road from pre-industrial production to well-developed State Capitalism (to say nothing of Communism) is so long that it cannot be traversed during an outbreak of revolutionary ardour ; and after such an outbreak there is usually a period during which demoralization and corruption are even more rampant than in normal times. An attempt to establish socialism in an undeveloped country, while the developed countries remain capitalistic, must pass through two phases, the first purely militant, in which the forces of internal and external capitalism are resisted, the second constructive, when the work of industrial development is undertaken under State management, and the population (probably with foreign help) is taught the more difficult parts of industrial processes. Russia is perhaps at the end of the militant phase, and has been successful so far as fighting is concerned ; but the constructive phase is a more difficult test. During the militant period, men's combative instincts as well as their nationalism assist the enthusiasm for a new economic order. But when peace is restored it becomes natural to want an easier life and to grow tired of everything strenuous and tense. At this moment the foreign capitalists, in their concessions, begin to offer all kinds of advantages, from well paid work for the ordinary wage-earner up to a fortune for the technical expert. To resist them by means of mere laws will be very difficult, as difficult as it has been found to prevent small private trading—an attempt which

Lenin frankly declares to have been a mistake. There is, it would seem, only one force which could keep communism up to the necessary pitch of enthusiasm, and that is nationalism, developing into imperialism as foreign aggressions are defeated. Otherwise the period during which revolutionary ardour can be kept alive will not be so long as the period required for the militant and constructive stages together. And if imperialism once gets the upper hand, it is of course vain to hope that any genuine communism can result. Marxians, who believe that economic causes alone operate in politics, ignore such difficulties as we have been considering, because they are psychological, not economic. But the difficulties are none the less real on that account. Nor is it safe for rulers to treat themselves, in the Bolshevik manner, as exempt from human weaknesses, not subject to psychological laws, and certain to retain their original purposes unchanged throughout any number of years of difficult power.

In spite of all these obstacles, the Bolsheviks *may* succeed ; and if they do, they may quite possibly become a model for China and India. There is one very important thing that they have made clear, and that is, that Socialism in undeveloped countries must be aristocratic, an affair of a few energetic intellectuals leading that small percentage of the population which consists of " class-conscious proletarians." It is impossible for progress in these countries to come as it has come in the West, because the men who are capable of leading revolutions have absorbed the latest Western thought, and will not be content with anything acknowledged to be out of date in England or France. Miliukov might have been content with a revolution like Cromwell's,

Kerensky with one like Danton's ; but the Bolsheviks, who alone had the energy required for success, wanted Marx's revolution, which Western revolutionaries still believed in because it had not yet happened. In the West, however, as in Marx's thought, his revolution had always been conceived as democratic. In Russia, where democracy is as yet impossible, some form of oligarchy had to be found until education could become more widespread, and this form of oligarchy was found in the dictatorship of the communist party. For the same reason, namely, that democracy is not yet possible in Russia, it was in the name of democracy that capitalism criticized and attacked the Bolsheviks. Thus both sides lost sight of an important part of the truth : the Bolsheviks, practically if not theoretically, of the fact that democracy is part of the aim of socialism ; their opponents, of the fact that democracy cannot be achieved all at once in an uneducated nation.

The Bolsheviks have, however, made a very important contribution to the solution of Eastern political problems by discovering an oligarchy which is neither that of birth nor that of wealth, but that of believers in a certain economic and political creed. When this creed is progressive and constructive, like that of the communists, it is likely to produce a better oligarchy than any other that is politically feasible, except for the one reason that it rouses the hostility of the outside world. This is, however, such a very large disadvantage that it is scarcely possible to strike the balance. If the governments of the Western Powers were socialistic, or even more or less neutral, there would be no such disadvantage. But while the wage-earners of England and America continue to elect as their chosen representatives men whose delight it is to oppress, starve and imprison all who advocate the interests of the wage-earners, less developed nations must reckon with our hostility, or with our insincere and corrupting friendship, as the price they have to pay for attempting any short cut to Socialism. It remains to be seen whether they can afford to pay the price.

We are thus brought back to international questions as dominating the problem of socialism in undeveloped countries. If Russia proves sufficiently strong and determined, if (what is unlikely but not impossible) China also comes in time to be dominated by communists, then—assuming Lenin's new methods successful in keeping the peasants contented—it is quite possible that Asia and Russia may be strong enough to succeed in a line of development displeasing to Europe and America, and ending in the establishment of their economic independence on a basis of socialism. But there are so many *ifs* in this argument that probability is against it. It is more probable that China will remain, and Russia will relapse, under the economic dominion of the Western Powers, until such time as their industry shall have been developed by capitalistic methods. In that case, the ultimate victory of Socialism, if it comes, will have to come from the advanced countries, as was universally assumed before the Russian Revolution. Whether and how socialism may be expected to come about in that case, we shall consider in the next chapter.

CHAPTER VII

SOCIALISM IN ADVANCED COUNTRIES

In the present chapter we have to examine the prospects for the ultimate success of socialism in advanced countries such as Great Britain, Germany and the United States. In these countries, all the conditions for the success of socialism already exist except the political ones : the wage-earners are educated and accustomed to industrial processes ; large-scale production, with all the necessary plant, is in being ; industrious habits have been taught in the stern school of capitalism. Moreover, it is just because of certain natural advantages that these countries are advanced : mineral wealth, geographical position, climate, and the character of the people are all in their favour as against the countries which are still undeveloped. Their methods of production being more efficient, they have vastly more wealth per head than Russia or China have ever had, and therefore they can afford a greater loss by disorganization and civil war without being reduced to absolute starvation. Apart from international difficulties, any one of these countries could become successfully socialistic to-morrow if it so desired. But the very success of capitalism in these countries, while producing the technical conditions for socialism, has also weakened the effective desire for it. No doubt the number of people calling themselves socialists has increased, but the intensity of their belief in their creed has diminished faster than their numbers have grown.

In a modern industrial country, the men who dictate policy and in effect constitute the government are the great capitalists. Even in pre-war Germany, where feudal survivals still had a certain strength, men like Krupp and Ballin had far more influence on policy than all the Junkers combined. In Great Britain and America, the power of the capitalists over the government is too obvious to need emphasis, although in both countries it is subject to certain limitations. Questions which vitally interest trade unions, such as those concerning wages and hours, are not always decided in England as capitalists desire; and in America popular pugnacity might precipitate a war with Japan against the wishes of Messrs. Morgan. But such exceptions to the power of the capitalists are few, since they can only arise over matters inspiring very widespread interest leading to opinions not dictated by the Press (which is, of course, merely a department of capitalist activities). The number of such questions may increase as education improves, or diminish as propaganda becomes more skilful. The art of advertisement, perfected by the competition of private capitalists, has given men a new skill in producing belief in absurd propositions. Those who have been successfully persuaded to believe in so-and-so's pills can obviously be led to believe in anything; accordingly, the same methods are used to make them adopt whatever view is to the interest of those who have most money to spend on advertisement, i.e. the great capitalists. Against these methods nothing will prevail permanently except intelligent scepticism—the very last thing that our education

is designed to produce. Is the situation then hopeless ?
Are we condemned for ever to a dictatorship of knaves
who mislead fools ? Or will the excess of advertisement produce as its own antidote a wholesome doubt
as to all frequently reiterated statements ?

There is, of course, one thing which discredits the
government, even with the most thoughtless, and
that is, defeat in war. This cause led to revolutions
in Russia, Germany, Austria and Hungary. Defeat
in war may therefore cause the overthrow of a government run in the interests of the capitalists, and replace
it by men who call themselves socialists. This
happened in Germany, but did not lead to socialism.
It is not a sufficient explanation of this fact to attribute
it, as the Russians do, to treachery in the leaders.
If nothing else had been involved, the rank and file
would have chosen other leaders. The German
communists, who wished actually to establish socialism,
were defeated because the majority of the nation
was against them, not because a handful of leaders
preferred power to consistency. The reason the
nation went against the communists was not any
abstract consideration of the merits of communism,
but merely the fact that the Allies could and would
prolong the starvation of Germany if they disliked
its economic policy. Ever since the Bolshevik revolution in Russia it has been an agreed policy among
all civilized governments that, if any nation adopts
communism, its inhabitants shall, if possible, be caused
to die of hunger until capitalism is restored,[1] while

---

[1] In 1921, at the height of the Russian famine, a scheme was
organized by philanthropists (not by Bolsheviks) to bring children
from the famine area to countries where food was plentiful.
Municipalities and others in England expressed willingness to
take these children, whose mothers sent the following appeal :
" We Russian mothers who are destined to die this winter from
starvation or disease implore the people of the whole world to

hordes of the most licentious soldiery available shall be let loose to rape, burn, murder and pillage until they are glutted.   In view of what was done in Hungary by the Rumanians after the fall of Bela Kun, it is small wonder if the Germans shrank from a similar experience.   If Russia had been able to give them food and military protection, their behaviour would probably have been very different.

Similar considerations would apply to any serious attempt at socialism in Great Britain, unless our commercial policy were radically changed before making the attempt.   Certain steps would, no doubt, be possible even now.   It would be possible to nationalize the railways and the mines if full compensation were paid.   It would be possible to make cautious approaches to self-government in industry, provided a first-rate conflict with capital could be avoided.   But such measures are only preparatory ; sooner or later, if socialism is to be introduced, there must be confiscation of private capital without compensation (though there might be, say, a life annuity to present holders).   Since capitalists perceive this, they will at some point make a stand, and prefer war to further concessions.   This may take the form of a capitalist government suppressing the workers, or of a capitalist opposition rebelling against a Labour

take our children from us, that those who are innocent may not share our horrible fate. We implore the world to do this because even at the cost of a voluntary and eternal separation, we long to repair the wrong we have committed in giving them a life which is worse than death. All of you who have children or who have lost children, in remembrance of the children who are dead and in the name of those who are still living, we beseech you ! Do not think of us ; we cannot be helped. We have lost all hope, but we shall yet be happy with the only happiness that a mother knows, in the knowledge that her chlid is safe." The Home Office rejected this appeal, and decreed that the children should be left to perish. (See *Daily Herald*, January 23, 1922.)

Government. Whichever form it takes, America, in its present mood, will, if necessary, interfere on the side of the capitalists. Without firing a shot, by merely prohibiting the exportation of cotton and wheat, the United States and Canada could bring us to our knees. We cannot therefore, as things stand at present, adopt any economic policy, even in home affairs, which is displeasing to our American masters. This is part of the price we have to pay for defeating Germany and blockading Russia; for if they were not ruined we should be less dependent upon America.

If Great Britain is to recover its former independence, and be able on occasion to defy the wishes of American millionaires, it will be necessary to restore the prosperity of Germany and Russia, mitigate the mutual enmities of the European Powers, find new sources of food supply in Hungary and South Russia, and do everything possible to bring about a United States of Europe. This would obviously be the right policy for the Labour Party, since capitalism is stronger in America than anywhere else, and liberation from America is the first condition of progress. France is, of course, the great obstacle to such a policy, since France wants to recover the position in Europe which she held in the time of Napoleon. But there are insuperable financial obstacles to the success of this policy, and it is possible that a sufficient money compensation would induce the French, after some experience of the difficulties, to abandon the endeavour to enslave Europe.

Unless France is brought to reason somehow, we have no alternative but to become the willing or unwilling allies of America, who may, in her present mood, compel us to join in a holy war against socialism whenever the trust magnates may deem it necessary. The right policy for Labour in these circumstances is clear. But unfortunately Labour is not in power.

The case of Germany has shown, and the case of Great Britain may show before long, that socialistic opinion easily gets the upper hand in a defeated and impoverished country, but that the actual establishment of socialism must begin in a country which is strong and rich—assuming that Russia is finally defeated by famine and financiers. If Russia could succeed, socialism might spread westward to Germany and Italy, might then be forced on France, and ultimately, in some watered-down form, be adopted in Great Britain. Russia, even in defeat, has a degree of strength and endurance which make such an hypothesis possible, though scarcely probable. But the other nations of Europe, since the war, are all dependent, directly or indirectly, upon the United States. If the Bolsheviks go under or cease to be socialists, the other nations of Europe must either fawn on the United States or form *inter se* a close economic, political and military alliance. This latter course would require some slight element of statesmanship in politicians, and in populations some power of forgetting old hatreds. If these are not forthcoming, Europe will be increasingly exploited by America, very likely to such an extent that almost its whole population will be converted to socialism. But that will not bring the downfall of capitalism any nearer, so long as we remain dependent upon America for our livelihood. America controls the world, and will continue to do so until Russia is prosperous and Europe united.

The future of mankind depends upon the action of America during the next half-century. If America advances smoothly upon the path of capitalistic imperialism which is indicated by present tendencies and opportunities, there will be a gradually increasing oppression of the rest of the world, a widening gulf between the wealth of the New World and the poverty of the Old, a growing hatred of America among the exploited nations, and at last, under socialist guidance, a world-wide revolt involving repudiation of all debts to America. Whether, in such a struggle, England would be on the side of America or on that of Europe and Asia, it is impossible to guess ; it would depend upon whether the Americans had thought our friendship or our trade the better worth securing. In either event, the war would probably be so long and so destructive that nothing would be left of European civilization at the end, while America itself would be reduced to poverty and might experience at home the socialism which had been crushed elsewhere. Thus a not improbable outcome would be a class war in America, leading to the destruction of industrialism, the death by starvation and disease of about half the population of the globe, and ultimately the return to a simpler manner of life. After reverting for centuries to the life of Red Indians, the Americans might be re-discovered by a second Columbus, hunting wild beasts with bows and arrows on Manhattan Island. Then the process would no doubt begin anew, reaching a similar futile culmination and a similar tragic collapse.

This is the prospect if American capitalism remains unrestrained in its career of exploitation. Industrialism tends to unify the world, and a half-century of victorious investments would make the United States the masters in every continent. They could not be resisted except in unison, and therefore the war provoked by their oppression would be world-wide. There are not only capitalist and proletarian individuals, but capitalist and proletarian nations. Since the war, America has been the capitalist nation *par excellence*, while we have sunk from first to second place. France belongs to the capitalist nations, not so much owing to her savings (which are largely dissipated), as owing to the fact that her products are mainly luxuries for the rich. Communism would probably greatly diminish the consumption of champagne and lace, and thus impoverish the poor in France as well as the rich. Germany, since the war, is a proletarian nation, and so are Russia and China. The Marxian class war, if it ever comes about, is more likely to be a war between capitalist and proletarian nations than a civil war between capitalists and proletarians in each country. A war between capitalist and proletarian nations would do no violence to nationalist instincts, and it is in proletarian nations that socialism has the best chance of spreading. There is therefore a very grave danger of such a world-wide clash as we have been compelled to foreshadow.

There are those, both among socialists and among capitalists, who contemplate a universal class war without horror. They feel confident that it will give the victory to their side, and that after that industrialism will run smoothly, grinding out happiness for the workers or wealth for the idle according to the taste of the particular war-monger. It is strange that, with the example of the late war before their eyes, there should still be people who imagine that a long and desperate war may sometimes bring what some of the belligerents desired. For whom did the late war end fortunately ? Krupps ? The Kaiser ?

The Tsar ? Mr. Asquith ? Sir Edward Grey ?
President Wilson ? Did any of these get out of the
war what they went into it to secure ? And how
about the young men who enlisted to end militarism
and make the world safe for democracy ? A war has
a momentum of its own, which is quite independent
of the wishes of those who set it going. To start
a war for an idealistic end is as absurd as it would
be to put a match to a ton of dynamite in hopes of
making toast at the resulting blaze. People are not
in fact always so silly as their idealistic war-talk
would make one suppose ; the noble ends that they
propose to themselves are often only a cloak (unconsciously worn as a rule) for their hatred and love
of carnage. That is why we hear so many noble
sentiments in war-time from men who were never
anything but obvious brutes in time of peace.

What was true of the late war would be true in a
far higher degree of a universal class war, because
it would be longer, more desperate, and of greater
extent. It may be taken as nearly certain that such
a war would not end in the establishment of either
capitalism or socialism, since both are forms of industrialism and both depend upon the existence of
a more or less civilized community. One may assume
that quite early in such a war all the most important
industrial plant would be blown up by traitors or
destroyed by bombs from aeroplanes ; that towns
or villages containing important works would be
asphyxiated by poison gases ; that navigation would
be made impossible ; and that ultimately almost
every one who was not a peasant would be killed by
war, famine or pestilence. The people who would
survive would be those backward agricultural populations which were too stupid or too uneducated to

understand what the war was about and too unimportant from the standpoint of production to invite the attention of the enemy. Enthusiastic communists (if any were left at the end of the war) would find these populations somewhat poor material with which to inaugurate the new era. Probably the village priests would get them hanged as atheists. The world might then have to wait a thousand years before their doctrines were heard of again.

Therefore, when we are considering the prospects of industrial civilization, a universal class war must be regarded as a dead end, not as the fiery gateway to a new world. We have to ask ourselves whether, short of such a catastrophe, there is any likelihood of the United States becoming socialistic, or at least neutral in the struggles between European socialists and capitalists. The question is grave, since, if Russia can be drawn into the orbit of American capitalism (as now seems probable), there is little hope of avoiding a complete collapse of civilization unless the American belief in capitalism can be shaken.

The organization of production in America is already such as scientific socialism requires. The main industrial products are produced monopolistically by the trusts, with a high degree of technical efficiency and an almost complete elimination of the waste involved in competition. Indeed, what Lenin calls State Capitalism may be said to exist already, since the State, for all practical purposes, is big business. Whoever thinks this statement exaggerated knows little of conditions in the United States. Take first the legislature. A Standard Oil multi-millionaire who desired a divorce went to live in Florida, had a very easy divorce law passed, was divorced under it, and

9

then had the law repealed.[1] The Tsar in the pleni-
tude of his power could not have done so well, since
the Church would have opposed him; but in
America such instances abound. Take next the
executive. It is customary in labour disputes for
the employers to hire private armies to fight strikers,
and to employ armoured trains to bomb the villages
inhabited by the wives and children of strikers. Nor
is the regular army unamenable to the orders of the
magnates. An official government inquiry reports a
prosecution where a certain decision was desired by
the champions of law and order, and where United
States troops surrounded the Court House and trained
cannon upon it in order to secure a verdict conform-
able to hundred-per-cent. Americanism.[2] (This was
before America's participation in the war.) As for
the judiciary, the way in which the big interests have
been able to use it has long been notorious.[3] And

[1] Upton Sinclair, *The Brass Check*, pp. 246–7.
[2] Final Report of the Commission on Industrial Relations (1915),
appointed by the United States Congress, p. 73.
[3] A good example is afforded by the Mooney case. See the
controversy between Mr. Beck, Solicitor-General of the United
States, and Mr. Frankfurter, of the Harvard Law School, in the
New Republic, January 18, 1922. The main facts of this case
are as follows :

On July 22, 1916, a bomb outrage occurred at San Francisco
during a parade in favour of military preparedness. Mooney,
whose political opinions were disliked by the police, was accused
of the crime (along with others). He was condemned to death,
chiefly on the testimony of a man named Oxman. Shortly after
his condemnation, it came out that Oxman had endeavoured to
induce another man to commit perjury in support of his (Oxman's)
testimony. This caused the judge who had condemned Mooney
to conclude that Oxman was not a reliable witness ; he therefore
urged that there should be a new trial. The case aroused world-
wide interest, and Kerensky's government urged President Wilson
to do what he could to prevent a miscarriage of justice. President
Wilson appointed a commission, which reported in favour of a
new trial. When it became clear that the evidence upon which
Mooney had been convicted was inadequate, and that he was in
all probability innocent, the Governor of California, instead of
allowing a new trial, commuted the sentence to imprisonment for

public opinion, being manufactured by the Press, is almost always on the side of the capitalists who control the newspapers. Thus the true government of the United States, at the present time, is an oligarchy of energetic multi-millionaires which controls an admirably efficient unified system of production. This system may fairly be described as State Capitalism. It differs from Socialism in two respects : one, that it is aristocratic ; the other, that it is run for the private profit of those who control it, not primarily for the profit of the community. It is in this last respect only that it differs from the system which the Bolsheviks are trying to create in Russia.

This system rouses at present a certain amount of discontent, but not so much as the economic systems of Europe. Broadly speaking, every class in America is more satisfied with its conditions than the corresponding class in Great Britain. What prospect is there that this general satisfaction will continue ?

Of course the chief reason why Americans are contented is that they are prosperous. Wages are on the whole higher than in this country, even taking into account the higher cost of living. The main causes of prosperity, in order of importance, seem to be the following : First, the immense natural resources of the country, together with the fact that

life. This punishment Mooney is still undergoing. Mr. Frankfurter, whose controversy with the Solicitor-General of the United States is referred to above, was a member of the commission appointed by President Wilson. The Solicitor-General's chief argument against him is that Frankfurter is not an Anglo-Saxon name, and that Mr. Frankfurter had better return to Austria, since " in the United States there is still—thank God—an old-fashioned hatred of anarchy and anarchists." In other words, such people have no right to a fair trial.

The case of Sacco and Vanzetti is equally instructive, and has also aroused world-wide indignation. The facts of this case are set forth in Colyer's *Americanism*, p. 102 ff.

it is not yet overcrowded. Secondly, the energy and ability of the capitalists. Thirdly, the absence of conservative traditions which is characteristic of a new country, making it possible to adopt more efficient technical methods than would be tolerated in Europe. Fourthly, the large immigration of adults, who give their work without the preliminary expense of infancy and education.

All these sources of prosperity are likely to diminish with the lapse of time. The natural resources will be to some degree exhausted, and the country will become more densely populated. The capitalists will tend more and more to be men who have inherited wealth instead of having acquired it themselves ; as this happens, they will come to display less energy and less ability. Conservative traditions may be expected to grow up as the population becomes more stabilized. Finally the immigration has already been restricted,[1] and must in any case bear a continually smaller ratio to the total as the native-born citizens grow more numerous. For all these reasons, the present advantages of the United States must be regarded as in part temporary.

Nevertheless, it is to be expected that the United States will continue for a long time to have more wealth per head than any European country. The possession of capital after the exhaustion produced elsewhere by the war would alone be sufficient to insure this. Unless, therefore, America were to

---

[1] It is true that the capitalists are endeavouring to get the restrictions relaxed. *The Times*, February 22, 1923, in a New York telegram, states : "The leaders of industry who appeared yesterday before the Senate Committee on immigration predicted economic disaster for the United States unless the immigration laws are changed so as to enlarge the sources of common labour." But it is unlikely that there will be a return to anything like the degree of freedom that prevailed before the war.

become involved in a long and unsuccessful war (which is unlikely), no widespread discontent is probable during the next few decades.

In spite of these considerations, there is reason to expect a gradual spread of socialism. What, more than anything else, has hitherto recommended the capitalist system to vigorous men in America is the fact that it gave everybody a chance to rise. So many very rich men started from humble beginnings that every man who had energy and intelligence could hope to become rich. Energy and intelligence are needed for successful socialist propaganda ; therefore such propaganda will not flourish while the men who could lead it find a career within the existing system. But the American capitalist system is rapidly crystallizing, and the opportunities of emerging from the ranks of the wage-earners grow less every year. As they grow less, men who have the same mentality as the Trust magnates without the same advantages will tend increasingly to criticize the capitalist system, and to regard as unfair the concentration of immense wealth and power in the hands of men whom they feel to be no better than themselves. Such men may be expected in time to rouse the ordinary wage-earner to a similar sense of injustice.

From the point of view of any man not possessed of large capital, the inherent reasonableness of socialism must come to recommend it as soon as great wealth has lost its glamour by being obviously unattainable. Socialism, in America, would not involve any serious change in the technical organization of business. When the capitalists at the head of the big trusts have become the sons or grandsons of the able men who created them, when they merely draw a huge income which they spend in idle dissipation, the work will have to be done by the administrative staff, who may be expected to despise their lazy masters. Socialism, at that stage, will merely mean turning the administrative staff into civil servants, and distributing the income of the useless millionaires among the employees. It is difficult to see what objection any class of employees could reasonably have to such a course of action. At present, the word "socialism" terrifies them, because they see visions of anarchy, murder and red rapine; they imagine gangs of hooligans invading their houses and nationalizing their wives, and they fear that they would have to live on *kasha* and black bread for the rest of their lives. But although human stupidity is certainly immense, it can hardly be sufficiently immense for such absurdities to go on being believed for ever. Without being formally renounced, they will lose their terrors, as hell-fire has done. Sooner or later, reason and self-interest combined must get the better of purely imaginary bogeys.

The spread of socialistic opinion in the United States is likely to be analogous to the spread of freethought in Europe. Official propaganda has been against freethought everywhere, and still is so in English-speaking countries. To this day, in England and America, practically all education involves religious propaganda, and an *avowed* freethinker cannot obtain any post in the teaching profession except a fellowship at two or three of the most advanced colleges at Oxford and Cambridge. Even in these exceptional places, absence of religion is a great handicap. Rewards, both in money and in honours, are largely closed to those who profess free opinions. George Meredith was not buried in Westminster Abbey because on one occasion he advocated terminable marriages. From top to bottom, every imaginable influence is brought to bear to induce freethinkers to conceal their opinions. The young are only allowed to be taught by hypocrites, because of the moral contamination to be feared from contact with honesty. Throughout the Continent, a much more severe pressure used to be exerted in the same sense, including active persecution.

Nevertheless, in France, Germany and Russia Christianity is now officially abandoned ; in England, active Christianity is practically confined to clergymen and maiden ladies ; and even in America religion is far less virulent than it was thirty years ago. This remarkable spread of freethought shows the powerlessness of official propaganda in the long run, when it is opposed to reason and common sense. Gradually the thing taught grows incredible, and even those who do not explicitly reject it are no longer influenced by it. Probably no one outside the China Inland Mission now believes that unbaptized children go to hell because Adam ate an apple. Very few believe in eternal punishment at all, and even those few could not name any particular person who will suffer everlasting torment, with the possible exception of Judas Iscariot. Belief in religion, even where it survives formally, has usually as little vitality or influence upon conduct as belief in the heptarchy and the Merovingian kings. When parsons fulminate against Sunday games, people merely think them silly, whereas in the Ages of Faith similar anathemas would have brought high and low, old and young, crawling on their stomachs to beg forgiveness of the priests. The whole of this change has come by the victory of reason over authority, and of obvious truth over motives of pecuniary self-interest.

In a very analogous way one may expect to see a belief in socialism, or at least a disbelief in capitalism, spread from individual to individual, by discussions in youth, by reading, and by disgust with the humbug and hypocrisy of those in power. It is in this way that the existing body of socialistic opinion has been built up, except in Russia, where, since the October revolution, the ecclesiastical and capitalistic methods of official propaganda have been applied to the manufacture of communists, with what success it would be hard to say. The Bolsheviks, and Western socialists who have fallen under their influence, attach far too much importance to official propaganda. They believe that the only way to make socialism popular is for the socialists, while still a small minority, to seize the State machine by some trick, and then apply the familiar methods of advertisement and frequently-repeated lies to the conversion of the populace. It is true that there is no other way of producing widespread belief in nonsense. If you manufacture a pill which the medical profession has publicly exposed as a fraud, only fools will believe that you are selling something valuable, and only foolish methods will win their belief. If you wish to persuade people that, because Adam ate an apple, all who have never heard of this interesting occurrence will be roasted in an everlasting fire by a benevolent Deity, you must catch them young, make them stupid by means of drink or athletics, and carefully isolate them from all contact with books or companions capable of making them think. If you wish to persuade people that a man who has inherited millions from his father, has never done a stroke of work in his life, and has divided his time between eating, drinking, and fornication, is drawing his income as " the reward of abstinence," and cannot be deprived of his wealth without crime and disaster to the body politic, you must inculcate from infancy a superstitious and snobbish reverence for the rich, a cowardly terror of the authorities, a lack of imagination which leads to the conviction that whatever exists is unchangeable, and, if possible, a belief that God is the all-wise cause of the follies of men. Such methods are essential for maintaining creeds which no sane man would accept without the influence of hypnotism. But no such methods are needed for the spread of opinions that accord with reason and common sense. Such opinions can spread, as freethought has done, by virtue of their own inherent attractiveness to vigorous and inquiring minds. The absurdity and injustice of the capitalist system are so obvious, as soon as the question is cleared of irrelevancies, that socialists have no need to rely upon irrational arguments or adopt the technique of spell-binders. The Bolsheviks, who have attempted to compress into months the work of decades and into a few years the work of generations, have been unable to rely upon the slow operation of reason. But such rapid work is unstable ; if the Russian communists fall, very few of the converts they have made since they acquired power will retain their present faith. The same methods which made it will unmake it, under the influence of a new set of propagandists. If socialism is to achieve a solid success, it must appeal to reason, not to the silly credulity which makes fools everywhere fit material for the schemes of knaves.

Socialists, as a rule, have been far too impatient. It is impatience that has inspired the doctrine of the class war, of the dictatorship of the communist party, and generally of force as opposed to reason.

I do not wish to exaggerate : no doubt *some* force will be needed. Force was needed to take the States of the Church away from the Pope, but only a very little force, because the work of persuasion had been adequately done beforehand. Force will be needed, at the last, to take the capital from the capitalists ; but it will be only a very little force, if all who will really profit by socialism have become persuaded of the fact. No one expects the vendors of patent medicines to accept the verdict of the medical profession, or the Pope and Cardinals to accept the verdict of science. Similarly no one can expect the trust magnates to accept the verdict of the socialists, even when they are the only people who still hold out. But when that time comes, when persuasion by means of reason has done all that it is capable of doing, the trust magnates will have become so weak that it will be possible to oust them with hardly more of a struggle than the police need in dealing with burglars. It is to this culmination, not to a bloody and doubtful class war, that socialist tactics ought to be directed.

It is in the United States, as the leading capitalist nation, that this reasonable propaganda of socialist opinion is most needed. But if it is to succeed, it must aim at a different division of classes from that which has hitherto dominated socialist oratory. It is not enough to win over the less well-paid industrial workers, who alone can find any appeal of self-interest in the current forms of socialism. It is necessary to win over the technical staff, since their sabotage (as appeared in Russia) can paralyse the machine in the first critical days of the new system. It is necessary to win over the agriculturists, in any country in which they form a large percentage, as they do in America. It is necessary to win over a considerable proportion of the professional classes and of the intellectuals, for fear of their hostile propaganda and obstruction. It is necessary to have such an overwhelming preponderance of force that there will be no need to fear destruction of capital, paralysis of industry, starvation, ferocity and disillusion—the familiar round of consequences from premature revolutions. In order to achieve all this, it is necessary to make it clear that the appeal is to reason rather than force, and that force will not be used until capitalists become a small band of turbulent rebels against democratically enacted laws. To make the appeal to reason successful among a sufficiently large section of the population, it will be necessary to abandon the class outlook hitherto prevailing among socialists, and to represent socialism as a gain to the community, not only to the wage-earners in the lower ranks of labour. The adoption of a class point of view breeds strife, oppression and bitterness, and cannot be expected to appeal to members of other classes. But if, as I firmly believe, a scientific socialism, careful to safeguard individual liberty as far as possible, and inaugurated without a long and disastrous war, is capable of increasing the happiness of all but an infinitesimal section in an advanced industrial community, it must be possible so to present the case for it that, apart from traditional prejudice, all but that infinitesimal section shall feel the force of the argument. It is in this way, and in this way only, that socialism can be made to prevail in a country like the United States. Some part of the argument as I see it will be set forth in the remaining chapters of this book.

PART II

CHAPTER VIII

WHAT MAKES A SOCIAL SYSTEM GOOD OR BAD?

I

ANY man who desires, as I do, a fundamental change in the structure of society is forced sooner or later to ask himself the question : what is it that makes one social system seem to him good and another bad ? This is undoubtedly very largely a matter of individual caprice. In history, for example, some prefer one epoch, some another. Some admire the polished and civilized ages, while others profess to admire the rude virtues of more barbarous times. One does not wish to think that one's political opinions result from mere fanciful preferences of this sort, yet I believe that an enormous proportion of political opinion comes, in the last analysis, from some untested, unexamined, almost unconscious love for a certain type of society actual or imagined. I think it is possible to arrive at something less subjective than such tastes and fancies, and I think the advocate of fundamental change, more obviously than any one else, needs to find ways of judging a social system which do not embody merely his individual tastes.

Men's proximate political opinions are defended by arguments—arguments as to the effect of this course or that : such a course will lead to war ; such another to economic slavery; such another to starvation. But in choosing the danger we most wish to avoid or the advantage we most wish to secure, we are almost all of us dominated by some more or less vague picture of the sort of society we should like to see existing. One man is not afraid of war, because he has a picture of Homeric heroes whose fighting he finds it agreeable to contemplate. Another is not afraid of economic slavery, because he thinks that he himself and his friends will be the slave-drivers rather than the slaves. Another is not afraid of starvation, because he has a secret hoard and therefore believes that privation brings out the latent heroism in men. And so they differ as to the course which is best to be pursued, and the grounds of their differences remain obscure to themselves and others. Being obscure, they are suitable subjects for endless quarrels. The only way to make people's political judgments more conscious, more explicit, and therefore more scientific, is to bring to the light of day the conception of an ideal society which underlies each man's opinion, and to discover, if we can, some method of comparing such ideals in respect of the universality, or otherwise, of their appeal.

I propose first of all to examine some ways of judging a social system which are common but which I believe to be erroneous, and then to suggest the ways in which I think such judgments should be formed.

Among most people at most times, the commonest way of judging is simply by inherited prejudices. Any society which is not in a state of rapid transition has customs and beliefs which have been handed down from previous generations, which are unquestioned, and which it appears utterly monstrous to go against. Such are the customs connected with religion, the family, property and so on. The peculiar merit of the Greeks was due largely to the fact that, being a commercial and seafaring people, they came across the customs and beliefs of innumerable and widely differing nations, and were thus led to a sceptical examination of the basis of all such customs, including their own. If my memory serves me, there is somewhere in Herodotus a story of a conversation between some Greeks and a barbarian tribe, in which the Greeks expressed horror of the barbarians for the practice of eating their dead, but the barbarians expressed quite equal horror of the practice of burying the dead, which to them was just as shocking as the other to the Greeks. Such experiences of intercourse with other nations diminish the hold which merely inherited beliefs have upon the man who lives in a fixed environment. In our age, this effect is produced not only by travel and commerce, but also by the changes in social custom inevitably caused by the growth of industrialism. Wherever industry is well developed and not very new, one finds that religion and the family, which are the twin props of every merely traditional social structure, lose their hold over men's minds. Consequently the force of tradition is less in the present age than it has ever been before. Nevertheless, it is even now as great probably as all other forces combined. Take, for example, the belief in the sacredness of private property—a belief bound up originally with the patriarchal family, the right which a man was supposed to have to the produce of his own labour, and the right which he was able to extort to what he had conquered by the sword. In spite of the antiquity and diminishing strength of these ancient grounds of belief in private property, and in spite of the fact that no new grounds are suggested,

10

the enormous majority of mankind have a deep and unquestioning belief in its sacredness, due largely to the taboo effect of the words " thou shalt not steal." It is clear that private property is an inheritance from the pre-industrial era when an individual man or family could make an individual product. In an industrial system a man never makes the whole of anything, but makes the thousandth part of a million things. Under these circumstances, it is totally absurd to say that a man has a right to the produce of his own labour. Consider a porter on a railway whose business it is to shunt goods trains : what proportion of the goods carried can be said to represent the produce of his labour ? The question is wholly insoluble. Therefore it is impossible to secure social justice by saying that each man shall have what he himself produces. Early socialists in the days before Marx were apt to suggest this as a cure for the injustices of capitalism, but their suggestions were both utopian and retrograde, since they were incompatible with large-scale industry. It is, therefore, evident that the injustice of capitalism cannot be cured so long as the sacredness of private property is recognized. The Bolsheviks have seen this and have, therefore, confiscated all private capital for the use of the State. It is because they have challenged men's belief in the sacredness of private property that the outcry against them has been so great. Even among professing socialists there are many who feel a thrill of horror at the thought of turning rich men out of their mansions in order to make room for overcrowded proletarians. Such instinctive feelings are difficult to overcome by mere reason. The few men who do so, like the leading Bolsheviks, have to face the hostility of the world. But by the actual creation of a social order which does not respect merely traditional prejudices, more is done to destroy such prejudices in ordinary minds than can be done by a century of theoretical propaganda. I believe it will appear, when time enables men to see things in due proportion, that the chief service of the Bolsheviks lies in their practical challenge to the belief in private property, a belief existing by no means only among the rich, and forming at the present time an obstacle to fundamental progress—so great an obstacle that only its destruction will make a better world possible.

Another thing which affects people's instinctive judgment of a social system, whether actual or imagined, is whether it would provide a career for the sort of person they think they are. One cannot imagine that Napoleon, even in youth, could have been very enthusiastic about dreams of universal peace ; or that captains of industry would be attracted by Samuel Butler's *Erewhon*, where all machines were illegal. Similarly, the artist will not enjoy the thought of a society where no man is allowed to paint unless his pictures are pleasing to the town council. And on this ground many artists are opponents of socialism. Men of science struggled against the system which existed in the seventeenth century and compelled them to teach nothing contradictory to revealed religion ; and in like manner intellectuals in Russia object to having to teach their subjects from a Marxian point of view. People who find a pleasure in ordering others about (and this includes most of the energetic people in the world) will not like anarchism, where every man can do as he pleases. They will be in rebellion against existing authority unless they are part of it, but will wish to replace it by their own authority, not to abolish it, because in a world where every man could do as he pleases, executive people would find no career. On the other hand, easy-going people will hate strenuous systems. They will oppose the setting-up of drill and severe educational methods. During the war, they called such things " Prussianism." If they were better informed about Russia, they would now call them " Bolshevism." I confess to a temperamental sympathy with this point of view, and my sympathy was confirmed by what I saw of China, the most easy-going country left in the world. But this is not an easy-going age, nor one in which such temperamental preferences can be allowed to weigh. It is an age in which we have to think less of the present than of the future, less of the lives of our own generation than of the lives they are preparing for the generations to come.

Another thing which influences people, more or less unconsciously, in their judgment as to a suggested social system, is the question whether the activities involved in the creating of it would be agreeable to them. I fear that revolutionaries are not always exempt from this motive. There are certainly some in whom hatred of the possessing classes is stronger than love for the dispossessed ; there are some to whom mere benevolent feeling appears to be repulsive humbug, and who derive the zeal of their revolutionary ardour mainly from the delight which they feel in the thought of punishing the bourgeoisie. Such men will, of course, always be found among the advocates of violent tactics, since without violence there is no satisfaction for their impulses. Patriotism and militarism have, in many men, a similar origin. The thought of fighting, or more probably, the thought of setting others to fight, is delightful to them, and patriotism recommends itself to them as a creed likely to produce fighting. I do not mean that men are conscious of these impulsive sources of their beliefs, but I do mean that such impulses operate in the kind of way studied by psycho-analysis, and I believe that it is of great importance to drag the operation of these impulses into the light of day, to be aware of their operation in ourselves and to do what we can to make others similarly aware ; for an underground, unconscious force operates against reason, eludes discussion, and makes objectivity impossible while it remains undetected.

Among writers of sociology and political theorists generally, a very common way of judging the social structure is by whether it constitutes a pleasant pattern to contemplate. Many social theorists forget that a community is composed of individuals, and that whatever of good or bad it may contain must be embodied in those individuals. They think of the State as something having a good of its own quite distinct from the good of the citizens ; and what they call the good of the State is usually, unconsciously to themselves, what gives them a certain aesthetic or moral satisfaction. We know that when God created the world he saw that it was good, obviously not from the point of view of the unfortunates who have to live in it, but from a higher point of view, presumably that of aesthetic contemplation. In like manner, social theorists create worlds in their imagination which they also see to be good in spite of the fact that they would be intolerable to live in. Such worlds are neat and tidy ; everybody does at each moment something which is in accordance with the central plan ; they obey the will of the administrator as the universe obeys the will of God. The theorist, of course, is always in imagination himself the administrator. This kind of social theory was made popular among professors by Hegel; it was used by him to laud the Prussian State, and has been used by his academic followers to support the conservatisms of their several countries. Since the war, the Hegelian theory has been at a discount, having been supposed in some mysterious way to have inspired the invasion of Belgium; but in other forms a similar outlook remains common. Much of the belief in industrialism, particularly as applied to backward countries, is of this sort; it is intolerable to the industrially minded to think of lazy populations sitting under banana-trees, eating the fruit as it drops, and being happy in unproductive idleness. Some forms of socialism are not free from this defect: they aim rather at creating the kind of State which is pleasing to theoretical contemplation than the kind which will suit with the temperaments of its citizens. A very great deal of imperialism is also of this sort; it is pleasant to see much of one's national colour on the map, and it is unpleasant to see one's dominions jagged and scattered owing to the intrusion of foreign territories. The habit of judging the State as it is to contemplate, not as it is to live in, arises from giving more importance to the faint and transient sentiments of an observer (when that observer happens to be oneself) than to the vivid and continual experiences of those who have to live under the government of the State. It is certainly a very potent source of bad social theory. Whoever wishes to be a social theorist should daily remind himself of the very simple, but important, maxim that a State is something in which people have to live, and not merely something to be read about in books, or contemplated as we contemplate the view from a mountain-top.

II

So far we have been concerned with ways of judging a society which we believe to be mistaken. It is time to turn to those to which we can assent.

There are two elements in a good society, namely : first, the present well-being of those who compose it, and secondly, its capacity for developing into something better. These two do not, by any means, always go together. Sometimes a society in which there is little present well-being may contain within itself the seeds of something better than any previous system. Sometimes, on the other hand, a society in which there is much diffused well-being may be unprogressive, for a time static, and ultimately decadent. It is, therefore, necessary to take account of both elements as independent ingredients of the sort of society we should wish to see existing. If the science of social dynamics were more developed and the art of prophecy less insecure, progressiveness would be a much more important quality in a society than present well-being. But politics is so far from scientific and the social future so very uncertain, that present well-being, which is indubitable, must be allowed as much weight as an uncertain future good, although this future good, if realized, will outweigh anything merely present because of its longer extension in time. " A bird in hand is worth two in the bush " —and this is particularly true when we are not sure there are any birds in the bush at all. Let us therefore begin with what makes the present well-being of a community.

In judging of the present well-being of a community, there are two opposite fallacies to be avoided. We may may call these, respectively, the fallacy of the aristocrat and the fallacy of the outside observer. We considered a moment ago the fallacy of the outside observer. The fallacy of the aristocrat consists in judging a society by the kind of life it affords to a privileged minority. The ancient empires of Egypt and Babylonia afforded a thoroughly agreeable existence for kings and priests and nobles, but the rest of the community were mostly slaves or serfs, and must have had an existence composed of unremitting toil and hardship. Modern capitalism affords a delightful existence for the captains of industry : for them there is adventure and free initiative, luxury and the admiration of contemporaries. But for the great mass of the workers there is merely a certain place in the great machine. To that place they are confined by the need of a livelihood, and no effective choice is open to them except the collective stopping of the whole machine by strikes or revolutions, which involve imminent risk of starvation. Defenders of the capitalist regime are apt to vaunt the liberty which it grants to men of enterprise, but this is an example of the aristocratic fallacy. In new countries, such as the United States used to be, and such as South America still is, there may be some truth in it, and therefore in such countries one sees capitalism at its best ; but in older countries whose resources are developed and whose population is nearly as great as present methods of industry can support, the supposed freedom of enterprise exists only for a few. The early history of railways in the United States is full of bold piratical adventures ; the railroad kings of that period remind one of Elizabethan buccaneers. But a railway in modern England is a very sober affair ; its capital is held largely by innumerable maiden ladies and orphans whose funds are administered by trustees, its directors are sleepy peers, its policy is traditional, and it does nothing to encourage new men with bold schemes. This is not due, as superficial observers suppose, to a difference between the British and American temperaments, but to a difference in their geography and industrial antiquity. But even taking the capitalist case at its best, even considering America as it was forty years ago, it was only the men of unusual enterprise and push and unscrupulousness who came to the top. Such men are, by definition, the minority, and a society which suits only them cannot be considered satisfactory except by one who commits the aristocratic fallacy. I am afraid there are many socialists who commit the same fallacy ; they imagine industry developed under State control, and they visualize themselves in that future millennium as part of the State control, not as part of the ordinary workaday labour. In a system of centralized bureaucratic State socialism, those who direct the machine will have all the advantages at present enjoyed by the captains of industry, with the exception of enormous wealth, which to a vigorous, executive and combative person is one of the smallest advantages of business success, being valued mainly as a tangible proof of ability and power and as a means of acquiring the respect of the herd. But it is not only the great captains of industry who will enjoy an exceptionally agreeable life under State socialism ; it is also the whole army of officials. It is obvious that the man who sits in a government office, and spends his time interfering with other people, has a pleasanter life than the man who works in a mine or stokes a liner. Yet there are many forms of socialism which would do nothing to remedy this inequality. The industrial machine as it has been developed by capitalism is full of injustices other than the inequality of wealth. Unless these other injustices are also remedied, a socialistic society may be scarcely pleasanter to the average manual worker than the existing system. This is concealed from labour politicians and from men with bureaucratic minds, because they envisage themselves in the new order as leaders or officials, not as ordinary workers. Their judgment of the society they aim at creating is, in fact, vitiated by the aristocratic fallacy. It may be that the evils of the present world must be cured one by one, that inequality of wealth must be tackled first, leaving inequality of power for a later stage, and inequality in the pleasantness of labour for perhaps a still later stage. It may be that a bureaucratic centralized State socialism is the necessary first step. It is not this that I am denying. What I am denying is that such a society is good in itself, and I do not think that any one who imagines with equal vividness the lives of all the members of the community can remain contented with an ideal which confines initiative, power, and the use of intelligence to a few.

A society which is to bring diffused well-being not only to one class or to one type of character, but as far as possible to every member of the community, must not be too systematic nor too orderly. It must not be the kind of society which a man of administrative temperament plans in his head and enforces by bayonets and the criminal law. Different individuals have different needs, and it is important to suit all needs that can be suited without damage to others. It is, of course, necessary to restrain predatory impulses. The insufficient amount of such restraint is one of the greatest evils of the world as it is. But it is at least equally disastrous to restrain creative impulses. This is the danger of what one may call tight systems.

A military machine or an industrial machine treats men as all alike, with the exception of the privileged few who direct it ; it has no room for other exceptions, no desire for the kind of work that would not be ordered from above, no toleration for the kind of person to whom it is difficult to become a mere cog in the machinery.

Perhaps the most important of all the qualities that a social system can possess, is that it must be such as people can *believe* in. Europe during the last five centuries has advanced with quite extraordinary rapidity in all that makes what we call civilization, but step by step with this advance has gone a progressive disintegration of belief. I do not mean merely belief in religious dogma, though this also has played its part. I mean belief in all the assumptions on which the social order is based ; all the sources of authority have become suspect and all inherited institutions have ceased to command assent. The war and the Russian Revolution gave the *coup de grâce* to such beliefs as remained. At the beginning of the war, democracy was still a fighting creed, something for which men were willing to die. At the end, poor President Wilson was left its one remaining votary, proclaiming his gospel in pathetic isolation to a world which shrugged its shoulders and went about its business as if he had not spoken. It may be that some element of injustice is essential to the existence of a social order, at any rate for many ages to come. But in ages of faith, men believe in the social order even when it makes them suffer, even when they are the victims of what to a later age appears unmerited misfortune. Nowadays this is not the case. The only men nowadays who believe in injustice are those who profit by it, and even they in their hearts feel that their belief is not genuine, but merely an embodiment of self-interest. I except from this indictment the big capitalists of America, who are more naïve, more untouched by modern thought than any other set of men, with the exception possibly of a few Central African negroes. American business men still believe in the capitalist system, but business men elsewhere merely hope it will last their lifetime, provided they can obtain sufficient machine guns and ships to shoot down or starve those who advocate systems which, in their hearts, they know to be better. Such half-hearted belief does not bring happiness. The capitalists tried to persuade themselves that their war against Russia was a holy crusade, but in this attempt they were very unsuccessful throughout Europe. And everybody except the capitalists is unable to create in himself even a semblance of belief in the old order, the order which made the war and blockaded Russia, the order which devastated Ireland, starves Germany and Austria, imprisons or kills socialists, and amid the tottering ruins of our old civilization, pursues the old absurd diplomatic game of haggling for territories and arming against nominally friendly nations. This old order is no longer capable of bringing happiness. It is not only its nominal victims who suffer, it is not only the defeated nations or the proletarians who find that life has lost its meaning. Even the well-to-do classes of Western Europe have no longer the sense of anything to live for. Having no purpose in life, they have plunged into a frantic pursuit of pleasure. But with every added pleasure comes added unhappiness ; while the senses are gratified, the soul remains hungry—there is no inward sense of well-being, but only futility and despair.

There is only one cure for this despair, and that is a faith that a man can believe. No man can be happy unless he feels his life in some way important; so long as his life remains a futile round of pleasures or pains leading to no end, realizing no purpose that he can believe to be of value, so long it is impossible to escape despair. In most men at the present time this despair is dumb and unconscious, and because it is unconscious, it cannot be avoided. It is like a spectre always looking over a man's shoulder and whispering acid words into his ear, but never seen, never looked at face to face. Once acknowledged, once faced, this despair can be coped with, but it can be coped with only by a new belief, by something which supersedes the search for pleasure. Although it may sound old-fashioned to say so, I do not believe that a tolerable existence is possible for an individual or a society without some sense of duty.

There is only one kind of duty that the modern man can acknowledge without superstition, and that is a duty to the community. There was a time when such ideals as God, country, family, could move men. That time is past. All such ideals were used by elderly rulers throughout the war to drive the young to slaughter each other in futile carnage. Most of the young at the time believed that the war was about something important, but now that it is nominally over, they see their mistake. Nothing good has come out of it except revolt against the system which caused it; the vices of the vanquished have been acquired by the victors, and the only new hope has come from Russia, the most defeated of all the nations in the great war. Socialism is, I believe, the only faith which can restore happiness to the world, which can cure it of the sickness left by the war, which can

give men the sense that their lives are capable of
something better than pleasure and can end the despair
that drives men to frivolous cruelty. The faith of
the Russian communists in the new thing they are
endeavouring to create is rather crude, rather ruthless,
possibly rather premature, but it makes their lives
happy as hardly any Western life is happy ; it enables
them to endure privations and dangers, and preserves
throughout a kind of joy and freshness in the soul
such as one does not find in the weary West. If there
were no other argument for socialism the fact that
it is a creative faith which the modern man can believe
would be alone enough to make it the hope of the
world.

And this brings me to the second of the two characteristics which a good society must have. It must be
progressive ; it must lead on to something still better.
Now fundamental progress seldom comes from those
who fit comfortably and easily into the existing system.
It is not, for example, from trust magnates that we
expect the inauguration of the new era. In like
manner, if we imagine socialism established, it will
not be from those who administer it or from those
who have least difficulty in adapting themselves to
it that new growth will come. New growth will
come from the creative people, the men of science,
the artists, the thinkers, many of whom very probably
will be critics of the new order. Under the influence
of commercialism, many men have come to think
that the important progress is progress in the technical
methods of production, better machinery, better
means of communication, and so on. This has been
true, since in the past labour was not sufficiently
productive to provide a good life for all. But it
is true no longer, and with our existing technical

knowledge, if we had a scientific socialist organization, every man could have enough without long hours of work. When once men have enough of material commodities, there is no great importance in providing them with a superfluity. It is only commercialism, the competitive struggle for markets, as reinforced by the luxury of the very rich, that has made mere quantity of goods seem so important. We have reached the point where we could organize our material resources in a way that would leave sufficiency and leisure for all. Therefore the important progress now is not in industrial production, but in ideas. One might hope that under socialism the energy liberated from the production of luxuries and armaments would be employed in the pursuit of knowledge and in the beautifying of life, bringing back for the many that artistic excellence which existed in the pre-industrial era for the few. But if this is to happen, there must be freedom for the creative people, the men of science and the artists. They must not be controlled at every point by State officials, or obliged to do work at every moment which is pleasing to existing prejudices. Without freedom, the man who is ahead of his age is rendered impotent. All innovations are, to begin with, displeasing to the majority, yet without innovations no society can progress. Freedom for exceptional people, provided their work is creative and not predatory, is the most important condition of progress in any society. There is always a tendency for the administrator to think of himself as God Almighty and to imagine himself capable of judging the good or bad in every new idea. This tendency is dangerous, and would be particularly dangerous in the earlier phases of socialism, where the administrator may be expected to have more power than he has ever had before. The danger can only be met by acknowledging the importance of creative work and the fact that the best creative work often does not commend itself to contemporaries. It is not in the least necessary that the artists and men of science should be rewarded for their work, since the best of them are indifferent to rewards and do their work merely because they love it. But it is necessary that they should be free to do it and free to make it known—that, for example, a man of science should be able to print his work without having first to find favour in the eyes of officials. All this will come about of itself if socialism comes as a liberation for the many, not as a punishment for the few, if it is love for the good we are creating that inspires us, and not merely hatred for the evil we are destroying. It would be demanding the impossible to suggest that hatred should be wholly absent as a generator of energy in the time of transition, but it is important that it should not be the fundamental motive. If hatred is the fundamental motive, the regime created will be oppressive and restrictive, not only where it must be, but also in many directions where oppression and restriction must be avoided if progress is not to cease. It is a world full of hope and joy that we must seek to create, not a world mainly designed to restrain men's evil impulses. Evil impulses must be restrained, especially during the time of transition while they are still strong, but this is an incidental part of our task, not its main purpose or inspiration. The main purpose and inspiration of any reconstruction which is to make a better world must be the liberation of creative impulses, so that men may see that out of them a happier life can be built than out of the present frantic struggle to seize and hold what others desire. Socialism once established may so regulate the material side of existence as to enable men to take it for granted and to leave their minds free to employ their leisure in those things which make the true glory of man.

CHAPTER IX

MORAL STANDARDS AND SOCIAL WELL-BEING

I

To anyone who reflects upon industrialism it is clear that it requires, for its successful practice, somewhat different virtues from those that were required in a pre-industrial community. But there is, to my mind, widespread misapprehension as to the nature of those virtues, owing to the fact that moralists confine their survey to a short period of time, and are more interested in the success of the individual than in that of the race. There is also, in all conventional moralists, a gross ignorance of psychology, making them unable to realize that certain virtues imply certain correlated vices, so that in recommending a virtue the consideration which ought to weigh is : Does this virtue, with its correlative vice, outweigh the opposite virtue with its correlative vice ? The fact that a virtue is good in itself is not enough ; it is necessary to take account of the vices that it entails and the virtues that it excludes.

I shall define as virtues those mental and physical habits which tend to produce a good community, and as vices those that tend to produce a bad one. Different people have different conceptions of what makes a community good or bad, and it is difficult to find arguments by which to establish the preferability of one's own conception. I cannot hope, therefore, to appeal to those whose tastes are very different from my own, but I hope and believe that there is nothing very singular in my own tastes. For my part, I should judge a community to be in a good state if I found a great deal of instinctive happiness, a prevalence of feelings of friendship and affection rather than hatred and envy, a capacity for creating and enjoying beauty, and the intellectual curiosity which leads to the advancement and diffusion of knowledge. I should judge a community to be in a bad state if I found much unhappiness from thwarted instinct, much hatred and envy, little sense of beauty, and little intellectual curiosity. As between these different elements of excellence or the reverse, I do not pretend to judge. Suppose, for the sake of argument, that intellectual curiosity and artistic capacity were found to be in some degree incompatible, I should find it difficult to say which ought to be preferred. But I should certainly think better of a community which contained something of both than of one which contained more of the one and none of the other. I do not, however, believe that there is any incompatibility among the four ingredients I have mentioned as constituting a good community, namely : happiness, friendship, enjoyment of beauty, and love of knowledge.

It is to be observed that I do not define as a virtue merely what leads to these good things for its possessor, but what leads to them for the community to which he belongs. For different purposes, the community that has to be considered is different. In the case of acts which have little effect outside the family, the family will be the community concerned. In the official actions of a mayor, the community concerned will be the municipality; in internal politics it will be the nation, and in foreign politics the world. Theoretically, it is always the whole world that is concerned, but practically the effects outside some limited circle are often negligible.

However moralists may recommend altruism, all the moral exhortations that have had widespread effects have appealed to purely selfish desires. Buddhism urged virtue on the ground that it led to Nirvana ; Christianity, on the ground that it led to heaven. In each of these great religions, virtue was that line of conduct which would be pursued by a prudent egoist. Neither of these, however, has much influence on the practical morality of our own time. For energetic people, the moral code of our time is that of "success"—the code which my generation learnt in childhood from Smiles's *Self-help*, and which modern young men learn from efficiency experts. In this code, "success" is defined as the acquisition of a large income. According to this code, it is wicked for a young man to be late at the office, even if what has delayed him is fetching the doctor for a sudden illness of his child ; but it is not wicked to oust a competitor by well-timed tale-bearing. Competition, hard work, and rigid self-control are demanded by this code ; .its rewards are dyspepsia and unutterable boredom, in all who have not a quite exceptional physique. By comparison with its votaries, St. Simeon Stylites was a voluptuary ; nevertheless they, like him, are pure egoists.

In sociology, we are concerned with men in the mass, not with rare and exceptional individuals. It is possible for a few saints to live a life which is in part unselfish, but it does not appear to be possible for the vast majority of mankind. The study of psychology, and more particularly of psycho-analysis, has torn aside the cloaks that our egoism wears, and has shown that when we think we are being unselfish, this is hardly ever in fact the case. It would therefore be useless to preach a morality which required unselfishness on the part of any large number of men. I do not think myself that there is any need to do so. Our natural impulses, properly directed and trained, are, I believe, capable of producing a good community, provided praise and blame are wisely apportioned.

It is through the operation of praise and blame that the positive morality of a community becomes socially effective. We all like praise and dislike blame ; moreover, rewards and punishments often accompany them. "Positive morality"—i.e. the habit of attaching praise to certain types of behaviour and blame to certain other types—has enormous influence on conduct. In Somaliland, and formerly among the aborigines of Formosa, a man was not thought sufficiently manly to deserve a wife until he had killed someone ; in fact, he was expected to bring the head of his victim to the wedding ceremony. The result was that even the mildest and gentlest of men, in obedience to the moral sense of the community, felt obliged to practise homicide. This custom is rapidly dying out among savages, but among the white races the same feeling persists as regards military service in war-time. Thus in spite of the egoism of human nature, the positive morality of neighbours forces men into conduct quite different from that which they would pursue if positive morality were different ; they even often sacrifice their lives for fear of being blamed. Positive morality is therefore a very tremendous power. I believe that at present it is quite unadapted to industrialism, and that it will have to be radically changed if industrialism is to survive.

There is one point in which the definition of virtue and vice given above departs from tradition and from common practice. We defined a virtue as a habit which tends to produce a good community, and a vice as one which tends to produce a bad community. In thus judging by results, we agreed in one important respect with the utilitarian school of moralists, among whom Bentham and the two Mills were the most eminent. The traditional view is different ; it holds that certain specified classes of actions are vicious, and that abstinence from all these is virtue. It is wicked to murder or steal (except on a large scale), it is wicked to speak ill of those in power, from the Deity to the policeman ; above all, it is wicked to have sexual intercourse outside marriage. These prohibitions may, in our degenerate age, be defended by utilitarian arguments, but in some cases—e.g. refusal of divorce for insanity—the utilitarian arguments are very far-fetched, and are obviously not what is really influencing the minds of those who use them. What is influencing their minds is the view that certain classes of acts are " wicked," quite independently of their consequences. I regard this view as superstitious, but it would take us too far from our theme to argue the question here. I shall therefore assume, without more ado, that actions are to be judged by the results to be expected from actions of that kind, and not by some supposed *a priori* moral code. I do not mean— what would be obviously impracticable—that we should habitually calculate the effects of our actions. What I mean is that, in deciding what sort of moral instruction should be given to the young, or what sort of actions should be punished by the criminal law, we should do our best to consider what sort of actions will promote or hinder the general well-being. It might almost seem as if this were a platitude. Yet a tremendous change would be effected if this platitude were acted upon. Our education, our criminal law, and our standards of praise and blame, would become completely different from what they are at present. How they would be altered, I shall now try to show.

Let us consider one by one the four kinds of excellence which we mentioned, beginning with instinctive happiness.

II

Instinctive Happiness.—I mean by this the sort of thing that is diminished by ill-health and destroyed by a bad liver, the kind of delight in life which one finds always more strongly developed in the young of any mammalian species than in the old. I doubt whether there is anything else that makes as much difference to the value of life from the point of view of the person who has to live it. Those who have instinctive delight in life are happy except when they have positive causes of unhappiness ; those who do not have it are unhappy except when they have positive causes of happiness. Moreover, outward causes of happiness have more effect upon those who delight in life, while those who do not are more affected by outward causes of unhappiness. Of all personal goods, delight in life is therefore the greatest ; and it is a condition for many others. I do not deny that it can be too dearly purchased, if it is obtained at the cost of injustice and stupidity. In the advanced industrial nations, apart from the agricultural population, I can think of only one small class that lives

so as to preserve it, namely, the male portion of the
British upper class. The public schools develop a
boy's physique at the expense of his intelligence
and sympathy; in this way, by the help of a good
income, he often succeeds in preserving instinctive
happiness. But the system is essentially aristocratic,
so that it cannot be regarded as in any degree a
contribution to the solution of our problem. Our
problem is to preserve instinctive happiness for the
many, not only for a privileged few.

The causes of instinctive happiness could best be
set forth by a medical man, but without medical
knowledge observation makes it easy to see broadly
what they are. Physical health and vigour come first,
but are obviously not alone sufficient. It is necessary
to have scope for instinctive desires, and also for
instinctive needs which often exist without corresponding explicit desires. Very few adults, whether
men or women, can preserve instinctive happiness in
a state of celibacy; this applies even to those women
who have no conscious desire for sexual satisfaction.
On this point, the evidence of psycho-analysis may
be taken as conclusive. Many women and some men
need also to have children sooner or later. To most
men, some kind of progressive career is important;
both to men and women, a certain amount of occupation
imposed by necessity, not chosen for its pleasurable
quality, is necessary for the avoidance of boredom.
But too much work and too little leisure are more
destructive of instinctive happiness than too little
work and too much leisure. Another essential is the
right amount of human companionship, neither too
much nor too little; but as to what is the right amount,
people vary greatly. Our instinctive nature seems to
be fairly adapted to the hunting stage, as may be seen

from the passion of rich men for shooting big game, killing birds, and careering after foxes. In the hunting stage, men had periods of violent exertion alternating with complete quiescence, while women had activities which were more continuous but less strenuous and less exciting. This probably accounts for the fact that men are more prone to gambling than women. One result of adaptation to the hunting stage is that most people like loud noise at times of excitement, alternating with silence at other times. In modern industrial life the noise is continuous, and this certainly has a debilitating nervous effect. I believe that almost everyone has a need (though often not a desire) for the sights and smells of the country. The delight of slum children on a country holiday is of a kind that points to the satisfaction of an instinctive need which urban life cannot supply. In recovering from a dangerous illness, the pleasure of being still alive consists mainly in joy in sunshine and the smell of rain and other such sensations familiar to primitive man.

The difference between needs and desires is important in the consideration of instinctive happiness. Our desires are mainly for things which primitive man did not get without difficulty : food and drink (especially the latter), leadership of the tribe, improvements in the methods of hunting and fighting. But we have many needs which are not associated with desires, because under primitive conditions these needs were always satisfied. Such are the needs of country sensations, of occasional silence and occasional solitude, of alternations of excitement and quiescence. To some extent, sex and maternity in women come under this head, because in a primitive community men see to the satisfaction of these feminine needs without any necessity for female co-operation. *Per contra*, there are desires which do not correspond to instinctive needs. The most important of these are the desires for drugs, including alcohol and tobacco. The fact that these desires are so readily stimulated by habit is an example of natural maladjustment from a Darwinian point of view. They differ from instinctive needs in two ways. First, from the point of view of survival, their satisfaction is not biologically useful ; drugs do not help a man either to survive himself or to have a numerous progeny. Secondly, from the psychological point of view, the craving that they satisfy depends upon the habit of taking them, not upon a pre-existent need. The instinctive dissatisfaction which leads a man to take to drink is usually something wholly unconnected with alcohol, such as business worries or disappointment in love. Drugs are a substitute for the thing instinctively needed, but an unsatisfactory substitute, because they never bring full instinctive satisfaction.[1]

With the advance of what is called civilization, our social and material environment has changed faster than our instincts, so that there has been an increasing discrepancy between the acts to which we are impelled by instinct and those to which we are constrained by prudence. Up to a point, this is quite unavoidable. Murder, robbery and rape are actions which may be prompted by instinct, but an orderly society must repress them. Work, especially when many are employed in one undertaking, requires regularity which is utterly contrary to our untrained nature. And although a man who followed his impulses in a state of nature would (at least in a cold climate) do

---

[1] I do not wish this to be regarded as an argument for prohibition, to which, on the whole, I am opposed.

a good deal of work in the course of an average day, yet it is very rare indeed that a man has any spontaneous impulse to the work which he has to do in a modern industrial community. He works for the sake of the pay, not because he likes the work. There are, of course, exceptions : artists, inventors, men of learning, healthy mothers who have few children and strong maternal instincts, people in positions of authority, a small percentage of sailors and peasants. But the exceptions are not sufficiently numerous to be an important section of the whole. The irksomeness of work has no doubt always existed since men took to agriculture ; it is mentioned in Genesis as a curse, and heaven has always been imagined as a place where no one does any work. But industrial methods have certainly made work more remote from instinct, and have destroyed the joy in craftsmanship which gave handicraftsmen something of the satisfaction of the artist. I do not think that, if industrial methods survive, we can hope to make the bulk of necessary work pleasant. The best we can hope is to diminish its amount, but there is no doubt that its amount could be diminished very greatly. It is chiefly in this direction that we must look for a lessening of the instinctive dissatisfaction involved in work.

A " return to nature," such as Rousseau's disciples dreamt of, is not possible without a complete break-up of our civilization. Regimentation, especially, is of the very essence of industrialism, which would necessarily perish without it. If this is an evil, and is unavoidable, our aim must be to have as little of it as is possible. This aim will be realized by making the hours of industrial labour as short as is compatible with the production of necessaries, and leaving the remaining hours of the day entirely untrammelled.

Four hours' boredom a day is a thing which most people could endure without damage ; and this is probably about what would be required.

In many other respects, the restraints upon instinct which now exist could be greatly diminished. Production at present has two correlative defects : that it is competitive, and that it is thought important to produce as much as possible. A great deal less work is required now to produce a given amount of goods than was required before the industrial revolution, and yet people live at higher pressure than they did then. This is chiefly due to competition. An immense amount of labour is wasted in getting orders and securing markets. At times when there is a great deal of unemployment, those who are not unemployed are overworked, because otherwise employers could not make a profit. The competitive management of industry for profit is the source of the trouble. For the same reason there is a desire to maximize production, because, with industrial methods, the production of immense quantities of a commodity is more capable of yielding a profit than the production of moderate quantities.[1] The whole urgency of the modern business world is towards speeding up, greater efficiency, more intense international competition, when it ought to be towards more ease, less hurry, and combination to produce goods for use rather than profit. Competition, since the industrial revolution, is an anachronism, leading inevitably to all the evils of the modern world.

The sense of strain, which is characteristic of all grades in an industrial community from the highest to the lowest, is due to instinctive maladjustment.

[1] Cf. R. Austin Freeman, *Social Decay and Regeneration* (Constable, 1921), esp. pp. 105-27.

Every kind of failure to satisfy deep instinctive needs produces strain, but the manifestations are somewhat different according to the instinct which is thwarted. The chief needs thwarted by industrialism, as at present conducted, are : the need of spontaneous and variable activities, the need of occasional quiet and solitude, and the need of contact with the earth. This applies to the working classes, but in the middle classes the thwarting of instinct is much more serious. A man who has any ambition cannot marry young, must be very careful how he has children, must if possible marry a girl whose father will help him professionally rather than a girl he likes, and when married must avoid infidelity, except so furtively as not to be found out. Our society is so imbued with the belief that happiness consists of financial success that men do not realize how much they are losing, and how much richer their lives might be if they cared less for money. But the results of their instinctive dissatisfaction are all the worse for being unconscious. Middle-class men, when they are no longer quite young, are generally filled with envy : envy of their more successful colleagues, envy of the young, and (strange as it may seem) envy of working-men. The result of the first kind of envy is to make them hostile to all intellectual or artistic eminence until it is so well-established that they dare not challenge it ; of the second, to make them rejoice in war because it gives them a chance to thwart the young who have to do the fighting ; of the third, to make them politically opposed to everything calculated to benefit wage-earners, such as education, sanitation, maintenance during unemployment, knowledge of birth control (which the middle class practise as a matter of course), housing reform, and so on. They believe that their opposition to these measures is based on economy and a desire to keep down the taxes, but in this they deceive themselves, because they do not object to the spending of vastly greater sums on armaments and wars. The same man often will object to the education rate on the ground that the poor have larger families than the well-to-do, and to birth control on the ground that it is immoral and unnatural except for those whose income is fairly comfortable. Men are strangely unconscious of their passions, and the envy which dominates most middle-aged professional men is a thing of which they know nothing, though the methods of psycho-analysis reveal it unerringly.

The failure of instinctive satisfaction in the wage-earning classes is less profound than in the professional classes, because, whatever Marxians may say, they have more freedom in the really important matters, such as marriage. Of course this greater freedom is being rapidly diminished by improvement in police methods, and by the continual tightening up of the " moral " standard through the activities of thwarted middle-class busybodies. This has gone so far that at present, in English law, the penalty for deserting a vindictive wife, if you are a wage-earner, is imprisonment for life.[1] In spite of this tendency, wage-earners, as yet, in good times, suffer less instinctive repression than professionals, because they are less dominated by respectability and snobbery. Nevertheless, the failure

[1] This fact is not generally known. The mechanism is as follows : The Court makes an order for maintenance, the wife makes a scandal where the man is employed, he is dismissed, cannot pay the maintenance, and is imprisoned for contempt of Court. He is legally liable for maintenance even while in prison : therefore on the very day he comes out his wife can have him put back for not paying maintenance during the period of his first imprisonment. And so it goes on until he dies or she is glutted with vengeance. This is not a fancy picture, as any one who knows prisoners can testify.

to satisfy instinctive needs is serious, particularly as regards spontaneity. The effect shows itself in love of excitement, thoughtless sentimentalism, and (in the more intelligent) hatred of richer people or of foreign nations.

It is evident that the first steps towards a cure for these evils are being taken by the trade unions, in those parts of their policy which are most criticized, such as restriction of output, refusal to believe that the only necessity is more production, shortening of hours, and so on. It is only by these methods that industrialism can be humanized and can realize the possibilities of good which are latent in it. It could be used to lighten physical labour, and to set men free for more agreeable activities. Hitherto, the competitive system has prevented its being so used. It should have made life more leisurely, but it has made it more hustling. Increase of leisure, diminution of hustle, are the ends to be sought, not mere quantitative increase of production. The trade unions have clearly perceived this, and have persisted in spite of lectures from every kind of middle- and upper-class pundit. This is one reason why there is more hope from self-government in industry than from State Socialism. The Bolsheviks, when they had established State Socialism, ranged themselves on the side of the worst capitalists on all the matters we have been considering. It is obvious that this must always be the case when conditions of work are determined bureaucratically by officials, instead of by the workers themselves.

III

Friendly Feeling.—It is impossible to find any single phrase to describe adequately the whole of what I wish to include under this head. I can, I think, best explain by avoiding hackneyed words which *seem* to convey the correct meaning but in fact fail to do so. An average human being is indifferent to the good or evil fortune of most other human beings, but has an emotional interest in a certain number of his fellow-creatures. This interest may involve pleasure in their good fortune and pain in their evil fortune ; or it may involve pain in their good fortune and pleasure in their evil fortune ; or it may involve one of these attitudes in certain respects and the other in certain other respects. I shall call these three attitudes friendly, hostile, and mixed, respectively. Broadly speaking, the second of the four goods which we wished to see realized in a community is the friendly attitude combined with as little as possible of the hostile attitude. But this is only a rough preliminary characterization of what I mean.

Biologically speaking, the purpose of life is to leave a large number of descendants. Our instincts, in the main, are such as would be likely to achieve this result in a rather uncivilized community. Biological success, in such a community, is achieved partly by co-operation, partly by competition. The former is promoted by friendly feeling, the latter by hostile feeling. Thus on the whole, we feel friendly towards those with whom it would be biologically advantageous to co-operate if we lived in uncivilized conditions, and hostile towards those with whom, in like conditions, it would pay us to compete. In all *genuine* friendship and hostility there is an instinctive basis connected with biological egoism (which includes the survival of descendants). Some religious teachers and moralists preach friendly feeling as a duty, but this only leads to hypocrisy. A great deal of morality is a cloak for hostility posing as "true kindness," and enabling the virtuous to think that in persecuting others out of their "vices" they are conferring a benefit. When I speak of friendly feeling I do not mean the sort that can be produced by preaching ; I mean the sort which is instinctive and spontaneous. There are two methods of increasing the amount of this kind of feeling. One is physiological, by regulating the action of the glands and the liver ; everyone knows that regular exercise makes one think better of other people. The other is economic and political, by producing a community in which the interests of different people harmonize as much as possible and as obviously as possible. Moral and religious teaching is supposed to be a third method, but this view seems to rest on a faulty psychology.

The stock instance of the friendly attitude is the feeling of a maternal mother for a young child. As the most obvious example of the unfriendly attitude we may take jealousy. Sex love is, of course, a good example of instinctive co-operation, since no one can have descendants without another's help. But in practice it is so hedged about by jealousy that, as a rule, it affords a less adequate example of friendly feeling than maternal affection. Paternal affection involves, as a rule, a mixed attitude. There is usually some genuine affection, but also much love of power, and much desire that children should reflect credit on their parents. A man will be pleased if his boy wins a prize at school, but displeased if he inherits money from his grandfather, so as to become independent of the paternal authority as soon as he is twenty-one. There is (in some) a melancholy satisfaction when one's boy dies for his country, of a sort not calculated to increase filial affection in those young men who witness it.

> Snug at the club two fathers sat,
> Cross, goggle-eyed, and full of chat.
> One of them said : " My eldest lad
> Writes cheery letters from Bagdad.
> But Arthur's getting all the fun
> At Arras with his nine-inch gun."
>
> " Yes," wheezed the other, " that's the luck !
> My boy's quite broken-hearted, stuck
> In England training all this year.
> Still, if there's truth in what we hear,
> The Huns intend to ask for more
>   Before they bolt across the Rhine."
> I watched them toddle through the door—
> These impotent old friends of mine.[1]

Of course, war affords the supreme example of instinctive co-operation and hostility. In war, the instinctive prime mover is hostility ; the friendly feeling towards our own side is derivative from hatred of the enemy. If we hear that some compatriot with whom we are acquainted has been captured by the enemy and brutally ill-used, we shall be full of sympathy, whereas if his brother dies a lingering death from cancer we shall take it as a mere statistical fact. If we hear that the enemy underfeed their prisoners, we shall feel genuine indignation, even if we are ourselves large employers paying wages which compel underfeeding. The formula is : sympathy with compatriots in all that they suffer through the common enemy, but indifference to all that they suffer from other causes. This shows that, as we asserted, the friendly feelings arising during war are derivative from the hostile ones, and could not exist in the same form or with the same widespread intensity if hatred

[1] *Fathers*, by Siegfried Sassoon. (*Counter-Attack*, p. 24, Heinemann, 1918.)

did not exist to stimulate them. Those who see in national co-operation during war an instinctive mechanism which could be applied to international co-operation during peace have failed to understand the nature of the mechanism which war brings into play, or the fact that without enmity there is no stimulus to set it in motion.

There is, it is true, in addition to sex and parenthood, a form of instinctive co-operation which involves no enemy, and looks at first sight very hopeful as a social incentive. I mean that kind of co-operation in work which, so far as human beings are concerned, one finds most developed among uncivilized peoples, and which is carried to its highest perfection by ants and bees. Rivers, in his book on *Instinct and the Unconscious* (p. 94 ff.) describes how the Melanesians carry out collective work apparently without any need of previous arrangements, by the help of the gregarious instinct. I do not believe, however, that much use can be made of this mechanism by civilized communities. The instinct involved appears to be very much weakened by civilization, and is probably incompatible with even the average degree of intellectual development that exists where school education is common. Moreover, even when it exists most strongly, it is not such as to make complicated large organizations possible. It seems also that with the progress of intelligence the individual grows more self-contained, less receptive to immediate impressions from other personalities, which survive chiefly in fragmentary and sporadic forms such as hypnotism. The primitive instinct for collective work is certainly one to be borne in mind, but I do not think it has any very important contribution to make to the solution of industrial problems.

In order to stimulate friendly feeling and diminish hostile feeling, the things that seem most important are : physical well-being, instinctive satisfaction, and absence of obvious conflict between the interests of different individuals or groups. On the first two heads, we have already said enough in considering instinctive happiness. The last head, however, raises some interesting points. Our present society, under the influence of liberal ideals, has become one which, while it retains immense social inequalities, leaves it open to any man to rise or sink in the social scale. This has resulted from combining capitalism with a measure of " equality of opportunity." In mediæval society the inequalities were as great as they are now, but they were stereotyped, and accepted by almost everybody as ordained by God. They did not therefore cause much envy, or much conflict between different classes. In the society that socialists aim at, there will not be inequality in material goods, and therefore economic competition and economic envy will be non-existent. But at present we have the evils of the mediæval system without its advantages : we have retained the injustices, while destroying the conception of life which made men tolerate them. It is evident that, if the prevalence of competition and envy is to be overcome, an economically stereo-typed society is essential. It is also evident that in the absence of the mediæval belief that hereditary social grades are of divine ordinance, the only stereo-typed society in which people can acquiesce is one which secures economic justice in an obvious form—that is to say, economic equality for all who are willing to work. Until that is secured, our economic system will continue to grind out hatred and ill-will. What is called "equality of opportunity" is, of course, not real equality, even of opportunity, so long as we retain inheritance of private property and better education for the children of the well-to-do. Inequality must breed strife unless it is supported by a philosophy or religion which even the unfortunate accept. At present, no such doctrine is conceivable. Therefore equality in material goods is an essential condition for the prevalence of friendly feelings between different classes, and even between the more fortunate and the less fortunate members of the same class, or between rivals who hope in time to outdistance each other. A society will not produce much in the way of mental goods unless it is materially stereotyped. I believe that this applies to all kinds of mental goods, but for the present it is only friendliness that concerns us.

In preaching the advantages of a materially stereotyped society, I am conscious of running counter to the real religion of our age—the religion of material progress. We think that it would be a great misfortune if the rate at which new mechanical inventions are made were to slacken, or if people were to grow lazy and easy-going. For my part, since I came to know China, I have come to regard " progress " and " efficiency " as the great misfortunes of the western world. I do not think it is worth while to preach difficult virtues or extremes of self-denial, because the response is not likely to be great. But I have hopes of laziness as a gospel. I think that if our education were strenuously directed to that end, by men with all the fierce energy produced by our present creed and way of life, it might be possible to induce people to be lazy. I do not mean that no one should work at all, but that few people should work more than is necessary for getting a living. At present, the leisure hours of a man's life are on the whole innocent, but his working hours, those for which he is paid (especially if he is highly paid), are as a rule harmful. If we were all lazy, and only worked under the spur of hunger, our whole society would be much happier. Think of a man like the late Lord Northcliffe, working like a galley-slave to produce bloodshed and misery on a scale hitherto unknown in human history. How admirable it would have been if he could have been persuaded to lie in the sun, or play bridge, or study chess-problems, or even take to drink. But, alas, such men have no vices.

IV

Enjoyment of Beauty.—On this subject it is not necessary to say much, as the defects of industrial civilization in this respect are generally recognized. It may, I think, be taken as agreed that industrialism, as it exists now, destroys beauty, creates ugliness, and tends to destroy artistic capacity. None of these are essential characteristics of industrialism. They spring from two sources : first, that industrialism is new and revolutionary ; secondly, that it is competitive and commercial. The result of the first is that people do not aim at permanence in industrial products, and are loath to lavish much care on something that may be superseded by to-morrow. The result of the second is that manufacturers value their wares, not for their intrinsic excellence, but for the profit to be made out of them, which is (roughly) the excess of their apparent value above what they are really worth, so that every defect not evident at first sight is advantageous to the producer. It is obvious that both these causes of ugliness might be expected to be absent from an industrialism which was stereotyped and socialistic, since it would be neither revolutionary nor worked for profit. It therefore remains only to consider the third point, namely, artistic capacity.

It would seem, from the history of art, that nine-tenths of artistic capacity, at least, depends upon tradition, and one-tenth, at most, upon individual merit. All the great flowering periods of art have come at the end of a slowly maturing tradition. There has, of course, been no time for industrialism to generate a tradition, and perhaps, if the absence of tradition were the only thing at fault, we could wait calmly for the operation of time. But I fear that the other element, individual artistic merit, without which no good tradition can be created, can hardly exist in an atmosphere of industrialized commercialism. Commerce which is not industrial is often extraordinarily favourable to art : Athens, Venice, Florence are noteworthy examples. But commerce which is industrial seems to have quite different artistic results. This comes probably from the utilitarian attitude which it generates. An artist is by temperament a person who sees things as they are in themselves, not in those rough convenient categories which serve for the business of life. To the ordinary man, grass is always green, but to the artist it is all sorts of different colours according to circumstances. This sort of thing, in anybody who is not already a famous artist, strikes the practical business man as a waste of time—it interferes with standardizing and cataloguing. The result is that, although eminent artists are fêted and highly-paid, the artistic attitude of mind is not tolerated in the young. A modern industrial community, when it wants an artist, has to import him from abroad ; it then pays him such vast sums that his head is turned and he begins to like money better than art. When the whole world has adopted commercial industrialism, the artistic habit of mind will everywhere be stamped out in youth by people who cannot see any value in it unless its possessor is already labelled as a celebrity. This points to the same requirements as we found before : a society which is stable as regards the material side of life and the methods of production, where industrialism has ceased to be competitive and is used to make life more leisurely instead of more strenuous. And the first step towards this end is the general diffusion of a less energetic conception of the good life.

Knowledge.—The strongest case for commercial industrialism can be made out under the head of scientific knowledge. Since the industrial revolution there has been an enormous increase both in the general level of education and in the number of men devoted to learning and research. The importance of science for industrial progress is very evident, and all industrial States encourage scientific research. But even in this sphere the utilitarian habit of mind inseparable from our present system has deleterious effects, which are only beginning to be evident. Unless some people love knowledge for its own sake, quite independently of its possible uses, the new discoveries will only concern the working-out of ideas inherited from disinterested investigators. Mendelism is now studied by hosts of agriculturists and stock-breeders, but Mendel was a monk who spent his leisure enjoying his peas-blossoms. A million years of practical agriculturists would never have discovered Mendelism. Wireless is of great practical importance : it facilitates slaughter in war, the dissemination of journalistic

falsehood in time of peace, and the broadcasting of
trivialities to relieve the tedium of evening hours not
devoted to success. But the men who made it possible
—Faraday, Maxwell and Hertz—were none of them
the least interested in furthering this remarkable
enrichment of human life ; they were men solely
interested in trying to understand physical processes,
and it can hardly be said that the existence of industrialism helped them even indirectly. The modern study
of the structure of the atom may have a profound
effect upon industrial processes, but those who are
engaged upon it are very little interested in this
possible future effect of their work. It seems likely
that the utilitarianism of commercial industry must
ultimately kill the pure desire for knowledge, just
as it kills the very analogous artistic impulse. In
America, where the more utilitarian aspects of science
are keenly appreciated, no great advance in pure theory
has been made. None of the fundamental discoveries
upon which practical applications depend have been
made in America. It seems probable that, as the
point of view appropriate to commercial industry
spreads, utilitarianism will make such fundamental
discoveries more and more rare, until at last those
who love knowledge for its own sake come to be
classified in youth as " morons " and kept in institutions
for harmless lunatics.

This, however, is not one of the main points I wish
to make. There are, in fact, two such points : first,
that pure science is infinitely more valuable than its
applications ; secondly, that its applications, so far,
have been in the main immeasurably harmful, and
will only cease to be so when men have a less strenuous
outlook on life.

To take the second point first : Science, hitherto,

has been used for three purposes : to increase the total production of commodities ; to make wars more destructive ; and to substitute trivial amusements for those that had some artistic or hygienic value. Increase in total production, though it had its importance a hundred years ago, has now become far less important than increase of leisure and the wise direction of production. On this point it is not necessary to enlarge further. The increasing destructiveness of wars also needs no comment. As for trivial amusements, think of the substitution of the cinema for the theatre ; think of the difference between the gramophone and the really beautiful songs of Russian peasants ; think of the difference between watching a great football match and playing in a small one. Owing to our belief that WORK is what matters, we have become unable to make our amusements anything but trivial. This is part of the price we had to pay for Puritanism ; it is no accident that the only great industrial countries are Protestant. People whose outlook on life is more leisurely have a higher standard for their amusements ; they like good plays, good music, and so on, not merely something that enables them to pass the time vacuously. So far, however, science has only intruded into the world of amusement in ways that have made it more trivial and less artistic. Nor can this be prevented so long as men think that only work is important.

As for the greater value of pure rather than applied science, that is a matter which goes deeper, but which it is difficult to argue. Applied science, while men retain their present ideals, has the sort of effects we have been considering, which I for my part find it very difficult to admire. Pure science—the understanding of natural processes, and the discovery of how the universe is constructed—seems to me the most god-like thing that men do. When I am tempted (as I often am) to wish the human race wiped out by some passing comet, I think of scientific knowledge and of art ; these two things seem to make our existence not wholly futile. But the *uses* of science, even at the best, are on a lower plane. A philosophy which values them more than science itself is gross, and cannot in the long run be otherwise than destructive of science.

On all four heads, therefore, we are led to the conclusion that our social system, our prevailing habits of mind, and our so-called moral ideals, are destructive of what is excellent. If excellence is to survive, we must become more leisurely, more just, less utilitarian, and less " progressive."

CHAPTER X

THE SOURCES OF POWER

I

THOSE who aim at any radical reform of our social system are faced by the difficulty that the existing system is advantageous to the holders of power, and is therefore difficult to change. It is not easy to see how power is to be wrested from those who now possess it, unless by a struggle so terrible as to destroy our whole civilization. The apparent hopelessness of this problem causes many to acquiesce in present evils in spite of keen consciousness of their magnitude, while it leads other to a recklessly revolutionary attitude which estranges those who have a sense of social responsibility. I believe that the problem is by no means as insoluble as it is thought to be. Power, even the most monarchical, requires a popular basis, either in the general opinion of some large group or in its traditions and habits. Tradition and habit, strong as they are, are diminishing forces in our kaleidoscopic world. Thus opinion becomes the decisive factor in determining who is to hold power in the future. This is the thesis which I wish to establish, by analysing the main sources of power in modern communities.

Power may be defined as ability to cause people to act as we wish, when they would have acted otherwise

but for the effects of our desires; it includes also
ability to prevent people from acting against our wishes,
which is sometimes the utmost that we aim at achieving
—for instance, in the case of a murderer who is executed.
A man possesses power in proportion to his capacity
for causing people to act in accordance with his
wishes, or for preventing them from acting otherwise.
The power of a group is similarly defined, by reference
to its collective or dominant wishes.

One may distinguish broadly two methods of
acquiring power, namely, force and persuasion. The
two are not sharply separated, and merge into each
other in marginal cases, but in most instances the
difference is clear : the power of the executioner over
his victim may be taken as the type of force, while
the power of a scientific discoverer over men's thoughts
may be taken as the type of persuasion. We may
set up the following definitions : *Force* is an influence
over the acts of others without altering their desires
and beliefs, or at any rate not by means of such
alteration ; *persuasion* is an influence over the acts
of others acquired by means of an alteration in their
desires or beliefs. But these definitions are not adequate to distinguish between force and persuasion in
doubtful cases. What shall we say of an influence
acquired through hypnotism or by supplying morphia ?
If we regard hypnotism as force, we must face the
fact that there is an element analogous to hypnotism
in almost all persuasion, and notably in early education. We cannot therefore draw any sharp line
between persuasion and force, or say precisely where
one ends and the other begins. But for practical
purposes the distinction is a useful one, and in most
cases it is not difficult to apply.

In politics there are two main forms of force. The

first is that applied in fighting, and also in the criminal law, except in so far as its penalties consist of fines. In this form, we make it physically impossible for a man to do things which we consider undesirable, either by putting him to death, or by depriving him of physical liberty. The second form of force is that which is applied in economic relations, and consists in the power of depriving a man of his livelihood in whole or part. I shall call the first form of force *military* (including force exercised by the police), and the second *economic*. Those who can exert military or economic force if they choose are the holders of military and economic power. Here again the distinction is by no means sharp. The pressure exerted on Germany during the war by the blockade was economic, but the power that made this pressure possible was in our sense military (i.e. naval). In international affairs the two kinds of power are constantly intermingled, but in the internal affairs of a country they are somewhat more clearly separated. A man can be starved by his employer or imprisoned by the magistrate, and these are, broadly speaking, two different forms of control to which he is subject. They merge into one when the law imprisons a man for having no visible means of subsistence.

We may therefore distinguish, though not too sharply, three kinds of power : military, economic, and mental. The power of armies and navies is military, the power of Trust magnates is economic, and the power of the Catholic Church is mental. I propose to consider in succession the sources of these three kinds of power, and I shall try to show that mental power is the ultimate source of the other two. If this is true, both military and economic power could be indefinitely modified by the operation of mental power.

II

Military Power.—There is one source of military power which seems at first sight accidental, but yet has almost more importance than any other ; I mean, the size of the national group concerned. Except in civil wars, military power is wielded by a national group, or by several nations in alliance. The size of a nation is determined by historical accidents which it seems impossible to rationalize. A nation is essentially a sentimental unit ; that is to say, its other forms of cohesion are based upon and caused by a unity of sentiment. It is true that, in certain modern instances (of which the United States is the chief), the unity of sentiment is derivative, in part, from the governmental unity, through the operation of education ; but even in such cases, the governmental unity was originally based upon a sentimental unity. The size of the sentimental unit, other things being equal, determines its military power. Thus any means of operating upon the sentiment of nationality may increase or decrease military power. The uniting of Germany under Bismarck is of course a stock instance.

The importance of mere size is hardly possible to exaggerate. In the seventeenth century, France defeated Holland, although the Dutch could almost certainly have defeated France if the populations of the two countries had been equal. Cromwell was capable, by his abilities, of playing just as great a part in the world as Napoleon, but was prevented by being at the head of a small nation instead of a large one. Nevertheless there are limits to the effect of size. Russia and China are not as strong as their numbers alone would lead us to expect. There are other sources of power in which they are deficient.

Apart from size, the most important source of military power is developed industry and access to mineral resources. The possession of mineral resources may be a matter of luck, involving no mental characteristics in the possessors. This might seem to militate against our contention that the sources of power are mental. But when a nation possesses minerals without industrial energy, they come to be controlled by others. This has happened in Spain and China; the Bolsheviks tried to prevent it in Russia, but it seems that they are to fail. Whoever may have the natural resources to begin with, they come sooner or later under the control of some energetic nation which is prepared to exploit them. The Japanese had hardly any natural advantages, but they made up for the deficiencies of their own resources by acquiring control of those of China. We may take it that a nation of sufficient size, if it has the necessary mental characteristics, will somehow acquire access to mineral resources. This is not, therefore, to be put among the pre-conditions of military power.

Developed industry, however, remains essential. It was mainly owing to deficiency in this respect that Russia came to grief. But although a certain degree of industrial development is necessary for munitions, sheer military strength may often turn the scale as between two nations which have both reached that minimum. I think that the British and the Americans are apt to under-estimate the influence of armies and navies. Take, for instance, the position at present (February 1923) as regards France, Germany and England. It is the practice among all parties to envelop this position in fine phrases, but the stark reality is as follows : France, by military force alone, has seized the Ruhr coalfield ; the Germans cannot resist because they are disarmed. Great Britain dislikes this policy, and also dislikes the repudiation by the French of their debt to us. If we possessed the necessary armaments, we should collect our debt from France by the same methods which the French are using against the Germans, or by a threat of these methods (if that proved sufficient). We do not do so because we are afraid of French aeroplanes. Thus the French, by means of armaments alone, have been enabled (*a*) to avoid paying their share of the cost of the great war ; (*b*) to seize the bulk of Germany's industrial resources. It might seem, therefore, that the investing of money in aeroplanes was abundantly justified as a business proposition.

The moral of this situation is that national power depends largely upon intelligence. The French, since the armistice (but for certain difficulties to be considered presently), have shown more intelligence than the British, because they have realized that superiority in weapons of destruction could be made a source of income, whereas we have been occupied in balancing our budget. An enormous proportion of the income of nations and individuals, nowadays, is blood-money : payment exacted by the threat of death. Therefore the most prudent nation is the nation which is in the best position to levy blackmail. I am not speaking figuratively ; I am stating sober truth. Those who still think in the commercial terms that were more or less applicable before the war are Rip van Winkles. Modern nations are highwaymen, saying to each other " your money or your life," and generally taking both.

One essential condition of great military power is capacity for public organization. This is a quality which is possessed in a high degree by a few nations but is very deficient in most. In some ways it is,

13

next to size, the most indispensable of all the conditions. In the second Punic war, the Romans were victorious mainly because of their superiority to the Carthaginians in this respect : Hannibal was not supported from home because of the jealousy of his government. The successes of the Germans in the earlier years of the war were mainly due to their superiority in this respect ; probably they surpassed all other nations, past and present, with the possible exception of the Japanese, in their powers of organizing for a national effort. The French, the British, and the Americans, all possess this power in a high degree ; the Italians and Austrians much less, the Russians still less, and the Chinese hardly at all.

It is obvious that capacity for public organization depends in the main upon psychological causes. Material causes, of course, enter in ; for example, easy communication and good railways. But these things are less important than the psychological factors. Canada and Australia are vast thinly-populated areas, yet there is no difficulty in organizing them for national purposes. The main qualities needed seem to be : strong collective desires for common ends ; a powerful but intellectualized herd-instinct ; and a willingness to subordinate one's own will to that of recognized leaders. The third of these qualities is lacking among educated Chinese, who also have less herd-instinct than most European nations. Uneducated Chinese have strong herd-instincts, but of a type which is too primitive for the needs of modern organization. An instance will make this clear. In 1922, there was a shipping strike among the Chinese seamen in Hong-Kong harbour. There was a first-class struggle, until at last almost the whole Chinese labouring population of Hong-Kong was drawn in on the side of the strikers. Failing to win by other methods, all the coolies, with their families, set to work to leave the town and seek a livelihood elsewhere. This was too much for the authorities, who felt compelled to give way. The whole incident was an admirable example of instinctive mass-action, but it would be fallacious to infer that a stable trade union organization could be built up among Chinese coolies at their present low educational level. Similar considerations apply to military organization.

Public organization is promoted by collective enthusiasm, and hindered by laziness and corruption. It is customary to regard laziness and corruption as vices, but in so far as they impair military efficiency they promote the welfare of mankind, and must therefore, to this extent, be reckoned as virtues. Usually, though not always, the collective passions of a large group are more harmful than individual passions ; therefore usually, though not always, the qualities that promote public organization are undesirable. But for the present we are not concerned with good and bad ; we are only considering, like Machiavelli, the sources of power. And among the sources of power, capacity for public organization must have a very high place.

Closely connected with capacity for public organization, though not identical with it, is another condition of military power : the existence of homogeneous passions throughout a large population. Great Britain was powerful against the Germans because the nation was united against them, but was impotent against the Bolsheviks because only the Government and the rich wished to defeat them. Even the most perfect organization breaks down if any considerable percentage of the people composing it are hostile to

its purpose. The two best examples of the victory
of organization against popular feeling are the Puritans
in the time of Cromwell and the Bolsheviks in our
own day ; the plan in each case was to organize those
who held certain opinions, while preventing the rest
of the population from developing counter-organiza-
tions. The Puritan experiment broke down by
treachery from within. The Bolshevik experiment is
still being tried so far as the *personnel* of the Government is concerned, but has been abandoned (at least
for the present) as regards its impersonal aim, namely,
the establishment of communism. Both these experi-
ments, as well as the failure of the British and French
Governments to suppress the Bolsheviks, point to the
impotence of organization when it is impeded by
conflicting passions. It has, however, immense power
in placing the merely indifferent at the disposal of the
Government. Most soldiers have no feeling either
for or against most wars, but the existence of military
organization makes them further the ends of those
who make wars, except in the rare cases when the
soldiers are actively hostile to these ends.

Hitherto we have been considering external military
power, but something must also be said as to the
internal power of governments, i.e. their capacity for
enforcing their will on their own subjects. In
revolutions, the limits to this capacity are exhibited
in a dramatic form, but they exist always and everywhere in less dramatic forms. It is generally recognized, for example, that Catholics cannot be forced
to obey laws which are contrary to their conscience.
It would be useless for the Government of India to
attempt to make Hindus eat beef or Mohammedans
eat pork. These are matters upon which average men
feel strongly. If they were equally opposed to work-

ing more than eight hours a day, or to being killed in a cause which does not interest them, governments would be equally powerless in these respects. But hitherto no population has felt as strongly about matters which affect its welfare as about trivial points of superstition. If a time should ever come when average men desired their own welfare, the ability of the State to enforce its will would be enormously curtailed.

The internal power of the State is, in theory, absolute, but in practice it is liable to many limitations. A measure desired by the Government may rouse such opposition as to cause revolution ; or it may so disorganize society as to weaken the nation dangerously in face of foreign enemies ; or it may wreck the economic machine by producing sabotage among employers or strikes among wage-earners. In these and other ways it may entail dangers which the Government dare not face. Thus a sufficiently powerful or determined group within a nation may be able to secure its own desires in spite of contrary desires on the part of the State.

What most weakens the power of the State is the organization of groups of citizens for common purposes other than those of the State. Churches, trade unions, and trusts are the principal examples in our day. The State has always shown jealousy of such organizations, and has always done all it dared to suppress them. Sometimes they have shown themselves stronger than the State, and have captured it. Constantine surrendered to the Church, and the American Government to the Trusts. The Bolsheviks and the closely analogous Fascisti are recent examples of organizations which captured the State. But what commonly happens is that such organizations merely impose certain restrictions upon what the State can do. In practice, when some question concerns a certain group much more intimately than it concerns any one else, it is generally possible for the group to get its own way in regard to that question, provided it is willing to organize and to suffer some degree of persecution. There are, of course, exceptions. The question whether Jews should be massacred concerns them more than any one else, yet in Poland they cannot get their own way as regards this question. The same may be said of the lynching of negroes and the police "frame-ups" against Reds in America. But these are matters arousing an exceptional degree of passion, and also involving race questions. Where race questions are not involved, a sufficiently determined minority will generally be able to hold its own against the State so far as its own affairs are concerned. It is in the highest degree desirable that this should be possible, and a State which treats minorities ruthlessly is *pro tanto* a bad State.

III

Economic Power.—I mean by economic power the ability to influence the conduct of others by increasing or diminishing their income or their means of livelihood. In an industrial community almost everybody has some degree of economic power over almost everybody else ; almost everybody could, with sufficient determination, find some means of damaging a given person financially. (The other form of economic power, by increasing a man's income, is, of course, only open to exceptional people—the rich, broadly speaking.) As production becomes more industrial, it becomes more organic, and therefore what one person does has more influence upon the fortune of another. Thus economic inter-dependence increases with the advance of industrialism.

But although every person may be able to damage every other, *given sufficient determination*, the amount of determination required is much greater for some than for others, and the amount of injury inflicted much less. So great is this discrepancy that, in ordinary quiet times, certain nations, and certain individuals within those nations, may be described as *the* holders of economic power. This comes about as follows :

The economic process from producer to consumer is partly co-operative, partly competitive. To take the latter first : competition, while it lasts, is injurious to both competitors, as compared to combination. It may, however, in the long run be advantageous to one of them, if it enables him to ruin his adversary and establish a monopoly at less cost than would have been involved in buying out his adversary. Thus, speaking generally, in all cases of competition economic power is on the side of the richer competitor—including in the estimate of his wealth all the credit that he is able to obtain. The more important cases of economic power, however, arise in the co-operative parts of the economic process. We may distinguish three main forms of economic co-operation : (1) that between different persons engaged in the same enterprise ; (2) that between different stages in the same process, e.g. between coal mining and the use of coal in iron foundries ; (3) that which occurs in trade, when the produce of one industry is exchanged for that of another. All these, in spite of the ill-will that occasionally arises between the parties, are forms of co-operation, because all are parts of the process of producing goods and supplying them to those who want them, and all are usually entered into from an expectation of mutual advantage. But although the advantage of co-operation is mutual, the disadvantage of a failure to co-operate is generally very much greater for one party than for the other. When that is the case, the party to whom failure matters least is at an advantage in bargaining, and therefore has more economic power than the other party. Where labour is unorganized, an employer suffers only a slight temporary inconvenience by refusing to engage a man who asks for work, whereas the man starves. The results of this inequality in bargaining power showed themselves in the early days of the industrial revolution in England, and may be seen to this day in Japan, or in China, where modern industry exists.

Of all forms of economic power, the most dominant is credit. There is, to the uninitiated, something mysterious about credit ; it seems like a mere book-keeping transaction, and yet it controls the lives of nations. If we are to understand it, we must get behind the book-keeping and see what it is that is really involved.

Credit, as the word implies, is primarily psychological : a person has credit when it is believed that if money is lent to him he will pay the interest. The person who must believe this is the person who has money to lend ; it is no use to have it believed by people who are poor. Lending money is, on the face of it, a mere paper transaction ; the moneylender does not give bags of gold to the borrower. From the point of view of economics, the important loans are of two sorts : those made to governments, and those made for productive enterprises. Let us take the latter first. Suppose a new railway is to be built. There are materials to be bought, operatives and staff to be paid, and directors who consider that their skill deserves remuneration. The goods which represent the wages and salaries of these people have to come from somewhere, and cannot come out of the receipts of the railway until the railway exists. The people who lend money for the construction of the railway are people whose income exceeds what they consider necessary expenditure, and who spend the excess on supplying goods to those who make the railway, in return for a promise of a certain proportion of the receipts to be earned by the railway when completed. Thus, apart from book-keeping, what happens when a man gives credit is that he parts with goods in the present in return for a promise of a certain amount of goods annually in perpetuity, or a larger amount for a specified period. In lending money to a State the process is essentially the same, except that the result the State is expected to show for the money is not a railway or any other useful product, but an adequate number of dead foreigners.

Different forms of credit differ greatly in the degree of power that the creditor acquires over the debtor. Take first the most important case, where the debtor is a State. Here we must distinguish according as the creditor is native or foreign. If the creditor is native his security is very poor. All the Continental States which were parties to the late war have repudiated all or most of their internal debt ; Russia has repudiated the whole, the others have repudiated the greater part by depreciating their currency. France partially repudiated in 1797 ; various States in the United States have repudiated at various times. A citizen who has lent to his own State has no hold over the debtor except that belonging to the plutocracy generally, namely, that, broadly speaking, they may assume that at most times the government will be run in their interests. But in times of crisis, such as the present, this assumption fails in many parts of the world, and those who have lent their money for the purpose of causing death find to their horror that they are allowed to die themselves.

The external creditor of a government is in a much stronger position. The security of the external creditor is the armies and navies of the most powerful countries among which creditors are to be found, together with the fact that a government which cannot borrow cannot conduct a serious war, so that every government tries to keep up its credit abroad. The French have repudiated their debt to us, and may before long be forced to repudiate their debt to the United States. If they do so, they will not be able to finance the war against Russia and Germany which they have in prospect. This is a serious matter, and shows that repudiation of external debt is very rash. The Russians repudiated their external debt, and their creditors caused a number of civil wars in Russia, culminating in a terrible famine. (I do not mean that there would have been no famine but for the creditors, but that, if they had permitted the re-organization of Russian transport, the evils of the famine could have been quite enormously mitigated.) The external creditor, as these examples show, has very powerful sanctions at his command, and will be paid unless a nation is either destitute or possessed of overwhelming military power.

The financial power of a State, including that of its nationals when they lend to foreigners, thus resolves itself, in the last analysis, into military power. The reason of this is that legal sanctions do not count for much as between States, and can in any case be abrogated by war. At the same time, a weak State, like Belgium, may acquire financial strength by alliance with a strong State like France. Military power is still the basis, but it may not be the military power of the State primarily concerned.

The whole of this system, however, is dependent upon a certain state of public opinion, and might alter completely if public opinion changed At present, if a State repudiates, the injured creditors cause it to be believed that the defaulting State has nationalized woman and instituted cannibalism ; the busybody morality of our time makes people regard this as a reason for fighting or boycotting the defaulting State ; and thus the virtuous are induced to give their lives to swell the ill-gotten gains of money-lenders. With a more enlightened public opinion, this would not happen, and the international power of financiers would be immensely lessened. Economic power is not something fatal and irresistible ; it is something generated by human beliefs and passions—absurd beliefs and destructive passions—and it could be entirely changed by different beliefs, which would stimulate different passions. Thus here again we come back to opinion as the ultimate source of power.

Within the limits of a single State, economic power has a legal basis, and is therefore somewhat different from economic power in the relations of different States or their nationals. In internal, as in external, economic relations, economic power very largely displays itself as control of credit, but credit is always based upon something more tangible.

Every person who controls something that others desire to possess or use or enjoy has, to that extent, economic power. It is not only the possession of capital that gives economic power. Chaliapin has made a comfortable income even in Soviet Russia, because he could refuse to sing, and people greatly desired to hear him sing. Of course, it would have been possible to threaten to shoot him, but it is doubtful whether this would have stimulated him to his best efforts : he happened to be in a peculiarly good position for sabotage. Most of those who live by their work are less fortunate, because they are not possessed of any rare form of skill ; but such wages as they get spring from the same source, namely, that the product of their work is desired. Their wages are increased by the desirability of their product, and diminished by the commonness of their skill. By combination, wage-earners can, theoretically, exact the advantages of monopoly, and extract as wages " all that the the traffic will bear." The fact that they get less than this is due to their failure to combine, especially internationally. But the fact that they get wages at all is proof that they have *some* economic power.

All economic products result from two factors only : land and labour—using the word "land" in the large sense of theoretical economics, so as to include water and mines and all the natural resources of the planet. Capital is not really a third factor. Capital is a product of the application of labour to land, and is merely a stage in production. Without land, human life is impossible ; without labour, very little human life would be possible. The power of capital is ultimately based upon the power of the landowner ; without his power, combinations of workers would be able to make their own capital and boycott the capital of the capitalist. The importance of this fact is, I think, insufficiently realized by some critics of the existing economic system, with the result that their criticisms antagonize an unnecessarily large proportion of the community. The excessive economic power of certain individuals rests, I believe, entirely on private owner-ship of land, natural resources, and legal monopolies. I shall try to show how this comes about.

In the complicated mechanism of production and sale, the greatest share of economic power belongs to those who can most easily dislocate the part of the mechanism affecting other people without bringing ruin upon themselves. It is evident that this advan-tage belongs to those parts of the total process which are best organized and easiest to subject to a single direction. It might be thought *a priori* that those who produce food would be in the strongest position, since no one can live without food. In chaotic conditions, such as those which have prevailed since the war in Russia and Austria, this is actually the case ; the peasant proprietor has advantages of the same kind (though on a smaller scale) as those that we are accustomed to associate with great financiers. He can withhold food from the towns, and so compel the government to negotiate with him as a co-equal power. But in normal times it is not the actual producer of food who is in the strongest position. It is necessary for him to sell his crop, and as he cannot sell direct to the consumer (who is usually distant and may be in another country), he has to sell to an intermediary. A big customer has advantages over a small one, so that the purchase of agricultural produce (except such as is perishable) tends to be in few hands. Again, if the produce has to travel by rail or sea, it cannot be advantageously handled by any person who is not favoured by the railway or the owners of the docks. Thus the big dealers in agri-cultural produce are likely to be . in alliance with railway and shipping interests. Yet again, most small-scale agriculturists, sooner or later, are obliged to raise a mortgage owing to the failure of their crop. The mortgage will be given them either by the railway or by the big dealer, or by a bank run in conjunction with the interests of the railway and the dealer. Thus the whole effective economic power connected with the production of food passes into the hands of financial magnates, whose control is derived from their possession or management of railways, docks, and credit.

One of the best illustrations of this process is the American Meat Trust. The following is an extract, on this subject, from the summary of the report of the Federal Trade Commissioner on the Meat Packing Industry, issued by The Federal Trade Commissioner at Washington on July 3, 1918. This extract is given in the report of the Committee on Trusts, 1919, reprinted 1922 [Cd. 9236], from which I have quoted it.

Five corporations—Armour and Co., Swift and Co., Morris and Co., Wilson and Co., Inc., and the Cudahy Packing Co.—hereafter referred to as the " Big Five " or " The Packers," together with their subsidiaries and affiliated companies, not only have a monopolistic control over the American meat-industry, but have secured control, similar in purpose if not yet in extent, over the principal substitutes for meat, such as eggs, cheese, and vegetable-oil products, and are rapidly extending their power to cover fish and nearly every kind of foodstuff.

In addition to these immense properties in the United States, the Armour, Swift, Morris and Wilson interests, either separately or jointly, own or control more than half of the export production of the Argentine, Brazil and Uruguay, and have large investments in other surplus meat-producing countries, including Australia. Under present shipping conditions the big American packers control more than half of the meat upon which the Allies are dependent.

The monopolistic position of the Big Five is based not only upon the large proportion of the meat business which they handle, ranging from 61 to 86 per cent. in the principal lines, but primarily upon their ownership, separately or jointly, of stockyards, car lines, cold-storage plants, branch houses, and the other essential facilities for the distribution of perishable foods.

The control of these five great corporations, furthermore, rests in the hands of a small group of individuals, namely, J. Ogden Armour, the Swift brothers, the Morris brothers, Thomas E. Wilson (acting under the veto of a small group of bankers), and the Cudahys.

A new and important aspect was added to the situation when the control of Sulzberger and Sons Co. (now known as Wilson and Co., Inc.) was secured, 1916, by a group of New York banks—Chase National Bank ; Guaranty Trust Co. ; Kuhn, Loeb and Co. ; William Salomon and Co. ; and Hallgarten and Co. The report of the Committee appointed by the House of Representatives to "investigate the concentration of control of money and credit " (the Pujo Committee) states (p. 59): "Morgan and Co. controls absolutely the Guaranty Trust Co." The Chase National Bank, a majority of its stock being owned by George F. Baker, is closely affiliated with the First National Bank. William Salomon and Co. and Hallgarten and Co. are closely affiliated with Kuhn, Loeb and Co. Thus we have three of the most powerful banking groups in the country, which the Pujo Committee classed among the six "most active agents in forwarding and bringing about the concentration of control of money and credit," now participating in the rapidly-maturing food monopoly above described. The entrance of the bankers into the packing business, it should also be noted, was not at all displeasing to the big packers. J. Ogden Armour and Louis F. Smith were frequently consulted during the negotiations, and Paul D. Cravath is quoted by Henry Veeder as giving assurance that the final arrangements would be "more than satisfactory " to Armour and Swift.

The menace of this concentrated control of the nation's food is increased by the fact that these five corporations and their five hundred and odd subsidiary, controlled, and affiliated companies are bound together by joint ownership, agreements, understandings, communities of interest, and family relationships.

The combination among the Big Five is not a casual agreement brought about by indirect and obscure methods, but a definite and positive conspiracy for the purpose of regulating purchases of live stock and controlling the price of meat, the terms of the conspiracy being found in certain documents which are in our possession.

There are undoubtedly rivalries in certain lines among the five corporations. Their agreements do not cover every phase of their manifold activities, nor is each of the five corporations a party to all agreements and understandings which exist. Each of the companies is free to secure advantages and profits for itself so long as it does not disturb the basic compact. Elaborate steps have been taken to disguise their real relations by maintaining a show of intense competition at the most conspicuous points of contact.

The Armour, Swift, Morris, and Wilson interests have entered into a combination with certain foreign corporations by which export shipments of beef, mutton, and other meats from the principal South American meat-producing countries are apportioned among the several companies on the basis of agreed percentages. In conjunction with this conspiracy, meetings are held for the purpose of securing the maintenance of the agreement and making such readjustments as from time to time may be desirable. The agreements restrict South American shipments to European countries and to the United States.

Since the meat supplies of North and South America constitute practically the only sources from which the United States and her Allies can satisfy their needs for their armies, navies, and civil populations, these two agreements constitute a conspiracy on the part of the Big Five, in conjunction with certain foreign corporations, to monopolize an essential of the food of the United States, England, France, and Italy.

The power of the Big Five in the United States has been, and is being, unfairly and illegally used to—

> Manipulate live stock markets ;
> Restrict inter-state and inter-national supplies of food ;
> Control the prices of dressed meats and other foods ;
> Defraud both the producers of food and consumers ;
> Crush effective competition ;
> Secure special privileges from railroads, stockyard companies, and municipalities ; and
> Profiteer.

The packers' profits in 1917 were more than four times as great as in the average year before the European war, although their sales in dollars and cents at even the inflated prices of last year had barely doubled. In the war years 1915–1916–1917 four of the five packers made net profits of $178,000,000.

Foreign Interests.—The investigation of the foreign interests of the American packers is not yet complete. The following

list of those companies which thus far have been identified
as subsidiary to or affiliated with the Big Five is indicative
of the extent of their activities abroad :—

Armour :—
Armour and Co. of Australia (Australia and New Zealand).
Armour and Co. of Uruguay (Uruguay).
Compania Armour do Brazil (Brazil).
Frigorifico Armour de la Plata (Argentine).
Dominion Tanneries (Ltd.) (Canada).
Armour Canadian Grain Co. (Canada).
Allen and Crom (Ltd.) (Great Britain).
Armour and Co. (Ltd.) (Great Britain).
Fowler Bros. (Ltd.) (Great Britain).
James Wright and Co. (Great Britain).
Times Cold Storage Co. (Great Britain).
Armour and Co. (Frankfort) (Germany).
Armour et Compagnie Société Anonyme (France).
Armour Societa Anonima Italiana (Italy).
Armour and Co. (Ltd.) (Denmark).

Armour and Morris :—
Sociedad Anonima La Blanca (Argentine).

Cudahy :—
Cudahy and Co. (Ltd.) (Australia).
The Cudahy Packing Co. (Ltd.) (Great Britain).

Morris :—
Morris Beef Co. (Ltd.) (Great Britain).
Haarers (Ltd.) (Great Britain).

Swift :—
Australian Meat Export Co. (Ltd.) (Australia).
Compania Swift do Brazil (Brazil).
Compania Swift de la Plata (Argentina).
Compania Swift de Montevideo (Uruguay).
Compania Paraguaya de Frigorifico (Paraguay).
Swift Canadian Co. (with its selling branches) (Canada).
Libby, McNeill and Libby of Canada (Canada).
Libby, McNeill and Libby of London (Great Britain).
Curry and Co. (Ltd.) (Great Britain).
Garner, Bennett and Co. (Ltd.) (Great Britain).
H. A. Lane and Co. (Ltd.) (Great Britain).
H. L. Swift Stall (Great Britain).
Swift Packing Co. (Ltd.) (France).
Franklin Land and Investment Co. (Great Britain).
Swift Beef Co. (Ltd.) (Great Britain).

Wilson :—

Frigorifico Wilson de la Argentine (Argentina).
Archer and Co. (Ltd.) (Great Britain).
Nuttall Provision Co. (Ltd.) (Great Britain).

In transmitting this report to the President of the United
States, the Federal Commission States :—

As we have followed these five great corporations through
their amazing and devious ramifications, followed them
through important branches of industry, of commerce, and
of finance—we have been able to trace back to its source
the great power which has made possible their growth. We
have found that it is not so much the means of production
and preparation, nor the sheer momentum of great wealth,
but the advantage which is obtained through a monopolistic
control of the market places and means of transportation
and distribution.

If these five great concerns owned no packing plants and
killed no cattle, and still retained control of the instruments
of transportation, of marketing, and of storage, their position
would not be less strong than it is.

The producer of live stock is at the mercy of these five
companies because they control the market facilities and,
to some extent, the rolling-stock which transports the product
to the market.

The competitors of these five concerns are at their mercy
because of the control of the market places, storage facilities,
and the refrigerator cars for distribution.

The consumer of meat products is at the mercy of these
five because both producer and competitor are helpless to
bring relief.

Those who wish to know how the vast power of
this Trust is used, without wishing to wade through
official documents, will do well to read *The Jungle*,
by Upton Sinclair. The similar power of the railway
over Californian agriculture some thirty years ago is
dealt with by Norris in *The Octopus*.

Where minerals are concerned, the process is different, both because, as a rule, they require expensive
plant to work them, and because a single mine or oil
well is a valuable property. For both these reasons,
there is nothing analogous to peasant proprietorship

where minerals are concerned, except in such cases as gold digging in a new goldfield. Apart from these rare exceptions, the working of minerals is in the hands of the big interests from the first. Those who own such things as iron, coal and oil are among the people with the greatest share of economic power. They are few in number, and can easily combine. Consequently, although oil is not more necessary to the world than wheat, the men who own oil are far more powerful than the men who grow wheat.

In the process which leads from producer to consumer, there are (so to speak) narrow passes through which the traffic must go, and those who control these passes have the greatest economic power. Suppose, gentle reader, that you were a highwayman, and wished to levy blackmail upon travellers. Travellers pass in small numbers along many roads to railway stations ; they all pass the ticket-collector on the way in and on the way out, and then disperse again to their several destinations. Therefore evidently the best post for a highwayman is that of ticket-collector. And that is precisely the view which our modern highwaymen take. In the case of minerals, the narrowest pass is at the start, and is bound up with ownership of the mine. In the case of grain, railways, docks and elevators are the pass. Sometimes, for example to some extent in the tobacco trade, the retailers have succeeded in capturing the most vital position. But in all advanced countries, and most of all in America, practically everything is controlled, at some stage, by the big interests.

It would be a mistake to regard this oligarchic organization of financial power as a law of nature. The reasons for it are psychological, and by no means unalterable. In Denmark, through co-operation, agriculture has been freed from the control of big business. Trade unions can give the wage-earner an equal voice with the capitalist, if not ultimately a greater voice. Every stage in the process from producer to consumer is equally necessary, but some are easier to organize. Those that are organized have an advantage over those that are not ; but if all stages were organized, as they might be, this advantage would cease. What is more important is that the excessive power of big business rests upon the law, since the law permits private ownership of natural and legal monopolies. The law rests upon opinion, and would be changed if a majority wished it changed. The fact that this change is not desired by a majority at present is due partly to tradition, partly to stupidity, partly to a snobbish reverence for the very rich. But tradition may die, stupidity may be dealt with by education, and snobbery towards the rich may grow less when people come to realize the price they pay for indulging it. Economic power, like military power, rests upon opinion. It would be impossible for the few to retain power over the many if the many genuinely desired to emancipate themselves. But this brings us to the third of the sources of power, namely, power over opinion. This source of power, as we have seen, is the basis of the others, and in the long run those who control opinion rule the world.

IV

Sources of Power over Opinion.—In all ages and places, the chief source of opinion is tradition : people believe what their fathers believed, with only such slight modifications as are absolutely thrust upon them. Tradition is mainly embodied in religion, and therefore priests, who represent religious tradition, tend to have great influence over opinion even in matters which are not specifically religious. Since religion rests almost wholly upon tradition, and is rejected by most people who have been able to free themselves in some degree from ancestral influences, those who stand for religion are likely to have a conservative cast of mind, and to defend ancient custom in every field. Moreover, religion, as it has come down to us, involves belief in authority, and therefore inclines men to submission to the powers that be. Since, further, the Churches own property which subversive people might be inclined to take away from them, they have every reason to oppose all manner of revolt. This no doubt accounts for the fact that they have defended every established atrocity after the conscience of average mankind had begun to rebel against it. In England, the Church objected to those who wanted to remove a few of the grossest abuses of the factory system. In America, it objected to abolitionists. In Belgium, it objected to agitation against the Congo atrocities, which was carried to a successful conclusion by the socialists. In France and Germany, before the war, the most bloodthirsty of all militarist journals were called respectively *La Croix* and *Die Kreuzzeitung*. Since the fourteenth century, the Church has consistently encouraged men's avarice and blood-lust, and discouraged every approach to humane and kindly feeling. There can be no doubt that, at any period during the last six hundred years, Christendom would have gained morally by the extinction of the Church.

This is still the case in our own day, and emancipation from the Churches is still an essential condition of improvement, particularly in America, where the Churches have more influence than in Europe. I think, however, that we may expect this emancipation to take place, provided those who desire it exert themselves to bring it about. Of all the requisites for the regeneration of our society, the decay of religion seems to me to have the best chance of being realized. I shall therefore waste no more words upon it, but shall proceed to the non-traditional sources of opinion.

An enormously powerful source of common opinion, particularly in politics, is the prestige of leaders. On most political questions, the average man has no view of his own. He chooses his party, either by tradition, or by general agreement with its aims in those matters about which he feels strongly. Having chosen his party, he acquires reverence for its leader, and is therefore willing to accept the leader's opinion on all matters about which he would otherwise be undecided. If Sir Edward Grey, on August 3, 1914, had pronounced in favour of neutrality, most Liberals in Great Britain would have accepted his view ; as it was, practically all accepted his decision in favour of intervention. When Disraeli pronounced against Protection, most Conservatives accepted his verdict ; when Joseph Chamberlain pronounced in favour of it, most of them accepted *his* verdict, though with some hesitation, because of the uncertainty of Mr. Arthur Balfour (as he then was). This makes it important to consider what determines the opinions of political leaders.

A political party represents, as a rule, certain interests which do not violently conflict with each other. Its policy is a compromise between the need of funds and the need of votes ; the former determines its acts, the latter its speeches. In a democracy, every party must seem to have something to offer to the average man. In a plutocracy, every ordinary party must *actually* have something to offer to some group of rich men, for the sake of its campaign fund. Therefore in a plutocratic democracy the leaders of most political parties must be hypocrites. The British Labour Party has happily escaped from this dilemma by obtaining its funds from the Trade Unions, but the Liberal Party has repeatedly given illustrations of the fact that its heart was where its treasure came from.

But in addition to these more or less gross causes, there is a subtler cause of divergence between the opinions of politicians and the interests of average men. Politicians, of whatever party, all have certain traits in common. To begin with, they all think politics important. This is the characteristic delusion of our time. Everybody knows the quotation in Gibbon[1] about how the Byzantine shopkeepers were interested in the most refined questions of theology. This strikes us as curious ; but the interest which we take in unimportant questions of politics is equally curious. In this we are encouraged by the politicians, who naturally imagine that they serve some useful purpose. Closely connected with this is another view which all politicians share, namely, that it is desirable that successful politicians should have a great deal of power. I believe the best social system to be one in which nobody has much power ; but it will be very difficult to induce politicians to establish such a system.

The better class of statesmen are liable to the fallacy of contemplating society, or their own nation, as a whole, and aiming at what they consider to be the interests of the whole as such, instead of conceiving the social system as something which contri-

[1] Chap. xxvii.

butes to the lives of a number of individuals, in whom alone anything either good or bad must be realized. For this reason, as well as for those previously given, the influence of politicians on opinion is apt to be bad.

In justice to a much-abused class of men, however, it should be admitted that the influence of public opinion on politicians is even worse. The badness of the Versailles Treaty is mainly attributable to the fact that Lloyd George was responsive to British public opinion, which at that time was utterly insane. It is said—I do not vouch for the story—that some-one expostulated with him when it was decided that the sum the Germans could pay was twenty-four thousand millions, and that he replied: "My dear fellow, if the General Election had lasted another fortnight, they would have been able to pay fifty thousand millions." In times of popular excitement, public opinion is generally worse than the opinion of poli-ticians, and those politicians who will not yield to it are swept away. The only possible cure for this, apart from education in scepticism, is to make the opera-tion of public opinion rather slow, so that a fit of excitement has time to pass off.

It will be said that the politicians were to blame for public opinion at the end of the war, since they had deliberately created it by war propaganda. This is no doubt partially true, but I think the effect of propaganda on opinion is sometimes exaggerated. However, propaganda must certainly be reckoned as one of the sources of power over opinion. We will therefore turn our attention to it.

It is clear that, if propaganda is to be effective, one side must get a better hearing than the other. If, when both sides offer propaganda, that of one side is selected by the bulk of the public, the result cannot be set down primarily to propaganda, since the public was evidently predisposed to one side. The *Daily Mail* acquired its circulation in spite of the competition of journals of every shade of opinion, therefore evidently it suited the popular taste better than they did. I am not thinking for the moment of propaganda among children, i.e. what is called education. I believe the effect of this to be very great, but I shall consider it later. For the present I am thinking of propaganda among adults. The chief effect of this is the same as that of a brass band : it does not make people alter their opinions, but it makes them hold their opinions more excitedly. I judge this from the fact that, in the main, people expose themselves to the propaganda that suits them, and are impervious to what does not suit them.[1] President Wilson noticed the propaganda of the " war for democracy," but did not notice the Bolshevik publication of the secret treaties. And the American nation followed suit. Since almost all the great disasters in politics come from the fact that people hold their opinions excitedly, propaganda must be reckoned an evil of the first magnitude ; but the evil is almost independent of the opinions advocated, since it consists in the passion which it causes to be associated with them. The disasters with which our civilization is faced are largely due to the fact that industrialism and education have given clever men vastly increased opportunities of producing collective excitement.

[1] This is only true in advanced countries. Consider, for example, the following paragraph, which appeared in the *Sunday Pictorial* : " The greatest single enterprise ever undertaken in the exhibition of motion pictures has been launched by an American corporation, formed for the purpose of flooding China with American films. This undertaking will, as a beginning, open 2,000 picture theatres in China. The propaganda possibilities of such an enterprise can hardly be over-estimated."

Education, as it exists at present, is subservient to Church or State or both, and therefore aims at producing credulity and servility—the two qualities upon which those institutions flourish. The fact that children usually continue through life to hold the religious opinions of their parents shows what a powerful force education is. It is certainly the main source of opinion wherever it is universal and compulsory. It is also the chief support of the existing State and of the financial oligarchy, both of which would quickly collapse if education attempted to make children think. I shall not now deal further with this topic, as I propose to consider it in a separate chapter. I shall only observe that the teachers, if they were sufficiently organized, could exact a great deal more intellectual freedom than they have at present. Their slavery, like that of other classes, could be cured by their own efforts, if they valued freedom more than money.

I come now to the last of the sources of opinion with which I propose to deal, namely, what may be called argument or reason. In our day it has become unfashionable to regard reason as a possible cause of a man's opinions. Freudians have persuaded intellectuals that all our opinions are expressions of obscure sexual passions, and Marxians have persuaded thoughtful wage-earners that all our opinions are products of our economic status. Pragmatists preach that the truth is what pays, and a commercial age has hailed this as a great gospel foreshadowed by the insight of advertisers. All these sects decry reason ; nevertheless all appeal to it. The Freudians believe that their doctrine of the importance of sex is not inspired, in themselves, by thwarted sexual impulses, but is the result of an impartial survey of the facts.

Marxians consider that Marx's doctrines are true, and are not merely evidence that he was hard up and had to come to the British Museum to keep warm. Pragmatists, in some sense, believe it to be objectively true that there is no objective truth, or at lowest believe it to be an absolute fact that pragmatism pays. There is therefore something which may be called reason, or the endeavour to discover truth, which even its professed critics really believe in. I believe that it has played a quite enormous part in the genesis of opinion, and that we must look to it, almost exclusively, for improvements in industrial civilization.

In the eighteenth century, belief in the power of reason was common. Voltaire, in one of his *Contes*, confronts his hero with a tribe of cannibals who are about to eat him. But he makes them a fine speech, beginning "Messieurs," and proves from first principles that it is a mistake to eat people. They are all converted, and acclaim him as a great man. The incident is of course intended to be comic, but nobody nowadays would imagine, even in fun, such a victory of reason. Rousseau and the Revolution put an end to this comfortable outlook, which, however, had a partial revival under the influence of nineteenth-century science. Science has since become either so technical as to be without interest for the man in the street, or so prostituted to interests and armaments as to be incapable of inspiring respect. Thus, although the results of science dominate us more and more, the scientific outlook upon the world has all but perished. This is infinitely to be regretted. But perhaps it is only a temporary eclipse.

It might be well to define "reason" before going farther. I do not mean by "reason" any faculty of determining the ends of life. The ends which a man will pursue are determined by his desires ; but he may pursue them wisely or unwisely. We may assume that the Kaiser hoped to increase his power by the war, and that the Tsar hoped to avert revolution ; neither of them showed wisdom in the choice of means to these ends. When I speak of "reason" I mean merely the endeavour to find out the truth about any matter with which we are concerned, as opposed to the endeavour to prove to ourselves that what we desire is true. At the beginning of the war, many men wished the war to break out, but continued, as before, to wish to grow rich. They therefore persuaded themselves that they would be enriched by the war, which only proved to be the case in a very small percentage of instances. Reason helps us to a right choice of means to our ends ; it also generates an impersonal habit of mind, since the truth is impersonal. On both grounds, it serves a useful purpose.

Those who believe that reason has little influence in human affairs are blind to many patent historical facts. Galileo had nothing but reason on his side in his contest with the Inquisition, yet Galileo's doctrine won the day. Modern science, which practically begins with him, has dominated human life more and more in each successive century. The doctrines that made the French Revolution, and the doctrines that made the Russian Revolution, had originally no force on their side except that of reason. The immense growth of socialism during the last hundred years must be attributed to the force of reason ; so must the extraordinary diminution in the power of the Churches. Most of the events of first-class importance in modern history, with the exception of the great war, have been contrary to the wishes of the Church, in spite of its unrivalled opportunities of propaganda and education. Men who genuinely believe in reason, and at the same time possess a vigorous intellect, have a power over opinion which is incalculable, because it is more lasting than any other power. It is to them and their influence that we must look if a better civilization is to emerge from the present chaos, not to a mixture of passion and propaganda leading to a dreary round of violence and disenchantment. To save the world requires faith and courage : faith in reason, and courage to proclaim what reason shows to be true. It is not a hopeless task to save the world, but it will never be achieved by those who allow themselves to think it hopeless.

CHAPTER XI

THE DISTRIBUTION OF POWER

I

In the last chapter we dealt with the sources of power, and found that, in the last analysis, they are all psychological. The power of a nation depends primarily upon its size, i.e. upon the number of people who have a homogeneous national sentiment; secondarily, upon its energy and capacity for public organization. Economic power within a nation depends upon combination by those who control some essential stage in the process of production and distribution; it can be checked by counter-organization, or destroyed by a change in the law. In the present chapter we shall be concerned with methods of bringing about a more even distribution of power. In theory, this problem was to have been solved by political democracy, but in practice it remains as acute as in the days of absolute monarchies.

In discussing this subject, we must distinguish between primary and secondary power, or ultimate and derivative power (as they may also be called). In the theory of government, there is a distinction between those who determine policy, and those who merely carry out a policy determined by others. In practice, as we shall see, this distinction is by no means sharp ; nevertheless it has a certain importance. The function of the Civil Service is different from that of Parliament, and the function of a general is different from that of his government which decides the issue of peace or war. We will therefore admit the distinction for the moment, and consider first the distribution of ultimate power.

In theory, ultimate power rests with those who choose the government, i.e. the electorate, in a democratic country. In international affairs, even in theory, ultimate power rests upon armed force ; but in the internal affairs of a State, it is supposed to depend upon the Constitution of the State concerned. This is, of course, only partially true. To begin with, questions of the greatest importance arise which were not foreseen when the Government was elected ; as to these, unless public opinion is strong and overwhelmingly on one side, the government has a free hand. In the second place, various sections of the community will not abide by the Constitution if the result annoys them beyond a point. In 1914, just before the outbreak of the war, many officers of the British army, with the support of the present Prime Minister, were engaged in mutiny because they disliked the Home Rule Bill. If a socialistic Parliament were to pass a measure (say) confiscating private property in land, a new Guy Fawkes, with the sanction of the whole Air Force, would blow it up, from above, not from below like his predecessor. In all developed industrial countries, the richer sections of the community regard themselves as above the law, and would resort to force if the law threatened to damage them seriously. The fact that they are capable of commanding force in excess of their numbers is one of which every progressive government has to take account, since it places a very real limitation upon the nominal powers of the democracy.

Apart from the possibility of unconstitutional resistance to the government, the rich have other weapons : bribery, direct and indirect ; control of propaganda ; the fact that the members of the government, even if not rich themselves, habitually associate with the rich ; and the financial embarrassments to which the government can be subjected if the rich think it worth while. For these reasons and many others, the actions of a government are always more friendly to the plutocracy than its professions at election time would have led the unwary to expect.

But it is not only the rich who have power over the government ; any strong and determined minority has a certain degree of influence. Trade unions have a certain degree of power ; the British Medical Association defeated Mr. Lloyd George over the Insurance Act. The Roman Catholics have power through their known inflexibility. Common soldiers and sailors have power when they refuse to fight, as in the English and French expeditions against the Bolsheviks. In considering democracy, it is necessary to take account of all these limitations to the nominally absolute power of the majority.

Confining ourselves as far as possible to primary power, do we wish to see an increase or a diminution in the power of groups to thwart the majority ? I have no doubt whatever that, in the best system, groups will have a great deal of control over all matters that primarily concern themselves. The modern State is so large and impersonal that its decisions as to any particular group are likely to be harsh and ignorant, unless the group in question is able to make its opinion effectively felt. There is grave danger of

persecution in the name of Majority, in cases where
the minority has some important contribution to make
to the life of the whole.   This applies most obviously
to the holders of unpopular opinions, and to racially
separate groups.   But it applies in some degree to
everybody, because everybody is in a minority on
some point.   The government might, for instance,
attack the trade unions one by one ; each single
trade union is a minority, but if they failed to stand
by each other the result would be disastrous to the
majority.   For these reasons and many others,
autonomy for groups as regards their own affairs is
of great importance.

There is, however, another side to this question.
The really powerful group, at the present day, is the
plutocracy.   The law allows freedom to this group,
not only as to matters primarily affecting themselves,
but as to matters of vital concern to others.   They
may, for instance, black-list men whose opinions they
dislike, and thereby cause these men to starve.   In
America, in spite of laws passed to prevent this, the
Courts hold that it is legal.[1]   The question as to
whether a certain issue primarily concerns one group
alone, or not, is always a difficult one, and in the case
of the plutocracy it is peculiarly so, because of the
widespread effects of their actions.   In any attempt to
diminish the personal power of the plutocrats by a
change in the economic system, it would be necessary
to reckon with their resistance, by every available
means, legal and illegal.   To deal with this situation
would need a strong government, centralized as in
war time.   This is the Bolshevik defence of what they
call the dictatorship of the proletariat.   If the argument
is unanswerable, socialism must begin by being State

[1] See Colyer, *Americanism* (Labour Publishing Co., 1922), p. 91.

socialism, and must be inaugurated by powerful bureaucrats with the mentality of military commanders. This prospect is unattractive, and I gravely doubt whether any good would come of socialism of such a type inaugurated in this manner. The power of the official in the new regime might be quite as disastrous as the power of the capitalist at present. But I do not believe that the Bolshevik argument is unanswerable. The power of the capitalist depends upon public opinion ; given a different opinion, the capitalist would be powerless, and his obstruction could be swept aside without difficulty. We need not therefore think in military terms when we are considering the distribution of power. We have only to persuade average men to claim their due share of power, instead of being content to live in servitude. When this has been adequately done, the actual transition will be easy.

The due distribution of primary power is to be obtained through democracy tempered by group autonomy. Autonomy for local groups having a separate local sentiment is a recognized principle of federal government. But there is need also of autonomy, in regard to specified purposes, for non-geographical groups to which these purposes are relevant.[1] It is not necessary that this autonomy should be formally recognized by the law, provided it is respected in practice. The Church of England is nominally subject to Parliament as regards its creeds and liturgy, but Parliament would not dream of imposing an alteration not desired by the Church, or of refusing one which was desired. This was not always the case ; in the sixteenth century, the government was

---

[1] On this subject see Harold J. Laski, *Authority in the Modern State* (Yale University Press, 1919), and *The Foundations of Sovereignty* (New York, 1921).

continually altering the beliefs of the clergy, the great majority of whom accepted the alterations passively. Gradually belief hardened in the clergy, while the government lost its interest in theology ; thus theological autonomy was bit by bit acquired in practice, without any change in the law. Churches might well have greater powers of self-government than they have. They might be allowed to determine the marriage law for their own members, on condition that they refrained henceforth from compelling others to submit to their superstitions. There is something to be said for allowing them complete control of the education of their own children, again on condition that they cease to interfere with the education of other people's children. These powers might belong to any religious body, defined as a collection of persons agreeing in their theological belief or unbelief. In the Near East, something of the sort has existed ever since the Mohammedan Conquest.

The application of this same principle of group-autonomy to industry is the source of the doctrines of guild socialism. This is a subject upon which there is a considerable literature, and it would over-weight one part of our subject to enter upon its niceties. I will only say, therefore, that an industry could win autonomy, in practice, by the same methods that have been practised by the Churches, and that I believe it very desirable that all the greater industries should do so. At the same time, it is clear, as Mr. Cole admits in his later writings, that if the producers are organized in autonomous guilds, the consumers also must have organizations to represent their interests, and cannot rely upon the State as representing the general body of all consumers. Associations of consumers are already fairly common. Apart from the co-operative movement, which tackles economic problems from the standpoint of the consumer, there are such bodies as the Railway Travellers' Protection Association, which organizes the consumers of railways, and the Automobile Association, which organizes the consumers of hotels.

Mr. Graham Wallas, in his book on *Our Social Heritage* (Allen & Unwin, 1921, pp. 103–119), advances several criticisms of guild socialism which seem to me, on their own plane, to be largely just, but to lose their applicability when taken in conjunction with the considerations advanced above in Chapter IX. His objections may be summarized under three heads : (1) that vocational organizations are technically conservative ; (2) that they tend to be jealous of any member who shows exceptional merit, and to aim at a dead uniformity ; (3) that they try to absorb into wages what might, as rent, be available for State revenue. I am not prepared to dispute any of these propositions, but I regard the first and third as positive arguments in favour of guild socialism, and the second as an argument of which it is easy to exaggerate the weight.

To begin with technical conservatism, I am convinced that a certain amount of this is desirable. At present, we pay too much attention to improvement of processes, and too little to those artistic considerations which only find scope within a stable tradition. Moreover, the amount of intelligence in a community is limited, and the part devoted to improving machines is taken away from improving life. Life might have gained by the technical advance in methods of production, but has not done so, and will not do so until laziness becomes a sufficient force to make men seek more leisure rather than more goods. This might easily be brought about by guild socialism. One may assume that the miners' guild, for instance, would receive orders from the State for a certain amount of coal, at a price fixed, as now, by bargaining ; and the amount ordered would, of course, depend upon the price agreed upon. It would rest with the guild whether to aim at much work and much pay, or at much leisure and less pay ; moreover, technical inefficiency could not sink beyond a certain point without destroying the opportunity for leisure. Such a system would afford a far stronger incentive than now exists for aiming at increase of leisure. So long as the present concentration of power lasts, technical advances are not to be desired, since they will be utilized mainly to increase oppression and war, owing to what we may call the " administrator's fallacy," i.e. the habit of aiming at some supposed good of the whole, rather than at the individual good of the separate citizens.

With regard to Mr. Wallas's second point, namely, that vocational organizations are hostile to merit and seek a dead uniformity, this is, I think, a real objection, so far as it goes. But for my part I do not think the organized industrial work of the world can be other than tedious and disagreeable to the great majority. It is to increased leisure, not to increased pleasure in work, that I look for improvement. The necessary minimum of labour may be done under somewhat unpleasant conditions, but it will leave many free hours every day for more congenial occupations.

As to the last of Mr. Wallas's points, namely, the difficulty of obtaining revenue if rent is absorbed by the guilds, that seems to be a powerful argument in favour of guild socialism. It used to be the custom among socialists, as it still is among communists, to look upon the State as the great hope of the future, and to think that a State freed from capitalism could safely be entrusted with a degree of power far surpassing that possessed by any State that has hitherto existed. I believe this to be an entire delusion, partly because it ignores the importance of minimizing power, partly because an organization which is merely geographical will give expression, in the main, to men's worst passions rather than to their best. The purposes of the State are in the main evil, and anything which makes it harder for the State to obtain money is a boon. About three-quarters of our revenue at present is spent on homicide, i.e. on paying for past wars and preparing for future ones. If we had more difficulty in raising taxes, we might have to give up flogging the Indians, bombing the inhabitants of Iraq from aeroplanes, stirring up civil wars in Russia, etc., etc. Mr. Lloyd George's main argument for giving self-government to Ireland was that it would save a shilling on the income tax. At present, the State is much worse morally than the average citizen, and this is largely because it is geographical. Therefore we ought to welcome any proposal which makes it harder for the State to get money, and at the same time transfers some of its powers to bodies which are not geographical.

The creation of organizations which are not geographical can, of course, be extended beyond the boundaries of a single State. There are important international organizations for postal and railway purposes ; banking and finance are largely international ; labour has the beginnings of an international organization, both politically and vocationally. It is probably easier to make gradual approaches to internationalism by means of international bodies for specific purposes than by such a machinery as the League of Nations. An international body in which each member represents a nation is likely to reproduce in its debates the diplomatic tug of war between the nations. If a genuinely international spirit is to exist, it is necessary that many of the members should represent, not nations, but international organizations such as the financiers or the miners.

The reason why the State gives expression to men's worst passions is that the State controls armaments and conducts wars and annexes territories. In the smaller countries of Northern Europe, such as Holland, Norway, Sweden and Denmark, the State does not have the bad qualities that it has in larger nations, because of the absence of effective military and naval power. But among the Great Powers, the State embodies primarily the lust for dominion. An organization can only give expression to those passions which the bulk of its members have in common ; therefore a geographical organization, such as the State, will mainly embody a man's geographical passions, of which the chief are hatred of foreigners and love of conquest. For this reason, if for no other, it is desirable that as much power as possible should belong to non-geographical organizations, which have at least a chance of embodying less ignoble passions.

As regards primary power, therefore, the conclusions to which we have been led are : That power should be lodged in different bodies for different purposes, and not concentrated, as at present, in the geographical State. Some powers are essentially geographical ; the most important of these is the power of making war. (A civil war which is not geographical cannot be a first-class modern war.)

Some functions which are essentially geographical demand as large an area as possible, notably tariffs, foreign policy, and war. Others are best delegated to smaller areas, especially where any strong local feeling exists. All powers which are not in essence geographical are likely to be better exercised by organizations of those interested. In general this can be secured without any change in the law, merely by determination on the part of such organizations. This method has advantages, since it leaves an ultimate control to the State whenever a sectional organization behaves so as to incur the active hostility of public opinion. Organizations for specific purposes are better when they are international than when they are national, provided they retain enough cohesion to be effective.

II

I come now to the problem of secondary power, i.e. the power of the official, taking that word in a large sense. Under the head of secondary power comes the power of generals and admirals (except when they mutiny), the power of civil servants, the power of trade union officials, the power of school-masters in so far as they are subject to an education authority, and the power of priests in so far as they have to submit to church discipline. Officials of big organizations such as railway companies also have secondary power. For practical purposes, we may confine ourselves to officials of various kinds.

The growth of organization in modern times has brought with it unavoidably a great increase in the power of officials. I have sometimes come across young men of an anarchistic tendency who imagined that it would be possible to dispense with officials altogether ; they had never asked themselves such questions as how a railway system could be run without a time-table, or how a time-table could be agreed upon without officials. Whenever a large number of people co-operate in a common task, which is an essential feature of industrialism, there must be officials to ensure the proper co-operation. Even a football team requires a captain. Many officials, with much secondary power, are absolutely essential to industrialism. It is possible to regret this fact, and to regard it as one of the evils of industrialism. But we cannot get rid of the multiplicity of officials except by getting rid of industrialism, and we cannot get rid of industrialism without causing about half of our present population to die of hunger. We must therefore seek methods of minimizing the evils of officialdom, since officialdom itself cannot be abolished.

Although the power of the official is derivative from higher authorities, his opportunities for the immediate exercise of power are likely to be greater than theirs. Unlike politicians and business men, he does not have to please the public in order to succeed ; he need only please his official superiors. He does this, not as a commercial traveller does, by bringing business, but by keeping business away. The result is a completely different set of virtues and vices from those of the enterprising man of business. On the one hand, he has no temptation to advertise shoddy wares, to practise the arts by which competitors are defeated, or to set others fighting in order to swell his dividends. On the other hand, he almost inevitably comes to regard the public as his enemy, because they interfere with the smooth working of routine ; he is engaged in a muted competition with his colleagues, conducted by the methods of the courtier, since its success depends upon winning the favour of individuals ; if he is honest and escapes all temptations to corruption, he is likely to fall a prey to love of power, and to develop a pleasure in thwarting outsiders who make complaints or suggest improvements. Since these outsiders usually know less of the detail of the question at issue than he does, he is tempted to use his knowledge obstructively, to puzzle and outwit the layman. For his daily happiness, it is only necessary to please the other people in the office ; hence all tend to hang together and support each other against the outside world. These defects of character are, of course, not universal ; some officials are genuinely zealous for the public good. But the situation of the official tends to promote these defects, which are pretty sure to show themselves when the human material is not above the average.

When the power of the official is fairly secure, his harmfulness is likely to be very great. I shall assume that he is honest, because honesty is a straightforward matter which can be secured in a straightforward way. The problem is to prevent the twin defects of red tape and vexatious interference. Take, for instance, education. A man or woman who is at the head of an educational institution in this country has to spend so much time filling up forms and keeping statistics that hardly any time is left for educating. No government office in the world remembers that the time spent in giving it information is time which might be spent in doing the work the office is supposed to promote. Probably English education would be improved if all government control were abolished beyond seeing that those in charge were capable and honest individuals ; and even this ought to be established once for all after a probationary period, and only reconsidered if serious scandals were to arise concerning the person in question. But this would not suit the officials, since it would diminish their power, and the exercise of power is sweet. Or again, take the police. In most countries the police regard it as their business to secure a verdict against any man whom they have charged, and cases are not infrequent where they have gone the length of perjury to prevent a colleague from being found out in a mistake.[1] If not enough crimes occur spontaneously, the police are apt to adopt the methods of the *agent provocateur,* so as to secure commendation for their zeal and skill in detecting the crimes they have caused. Everyone remembers the case of Azev in Tsarist Russia, who was simultaneously head of the secret police and head of the social revolutionaries, and who pleased both sides equally by the organizing of assassinations and the detection of the assassins, until an ex-Minister, sore at being dismissed, betrayed him. This is what bureaucracy leads to when it is unchecked.

It is clear that what is needed is some method of bringing the official effectively under the control of public opinion, especially the public opinion of those

---

[1] The following incident (*Daily Herald,* April 12, 1922) is not so exceptional as could be wished : " I have just been hearing details of the case at Kingston yesterday when a picket was charged with assaulting the police. W. H. Thompson, who defended, insisted that all the witnesses should be turned out of the court, including the police-constable who complained that he had been assaulted. Consequently, practically every witness contradicted every other witness. But the cream of the joke came when the constable himself was in the box. ' You made notes of this at the time ? ' W. H. Thompson inquired. The P.C. replied in the affirmative. ' When and where did you make notes ? ' ' In my note-book at the time,' and the witness drew it from his pocket. ' I'd like to have a look at that book,' the solicitor remarked. There was a good deal of protest, but W. H. Thompson is a persistent person. He got the book, and *there was no single note of the occurrence at all.*"

most affected by his actions. There are, however, two difficulties : first, that some degree of permanence is necessary to the technical efficiency of the official and to attract able men ; secondly, that the official is in theory (and sometimes in practice) the representative of the public as against sectional interests. If the Treasury aimed at popularity, the country would be bankrupt in six months. There are unanswerable reasons for giving to certain officials a status which will enable them to defy foolish or factious criticism. The problem of combining these two opposite needs is by no means a simple one.

In America, under the influence of democratic theory, an attempt was made to bring the official under the control of public opinion by means of the spoils system, which gave all government posts, down to the lowest, to party men, who changed whenever the government changed. This, of course, merely substituted the evils of politics for those of officialdom ; and in the Civil Service the evils of politics are certainly the greater of the two. If an official is to be made in some way amenable to public opinion, it must not be party political opinion, and must not be influenced by party considerations. Probably certain officials, such as those in the Treasury, ought to remain as aloof as they are at present, since they must be unpopular if they perform their duties adequately. For others, some method other than the spoils system must be found, if their characteristic faults are to be prevented without being replaced by faults that are still worse.

A more hopeful method is by means of vocational constituencies. A trade union official will usually, in the main, consider the interests of his trade union, because the business with which he is concerned touches his constituents nearly, and has to do with matters as to which they have the knowledge that comes of experience. The position of (say) a railway official under state socialism would not be analogous. It is true that the ultimate power would rest with the people, but not with a specially well-informed section of the people. Moreover, there would be so many intermediate stages between the primary power of the people and the executive power of the official that the official would not, in practice, be subject to any democratic control except in the rare issues that arouse strong public feeling. The effective control over an official would be that of his official superiors, the bulk of whom would aim only at an easy life, while the few with exceptional public spirit would harry and regiment the users of railways under the illusion that they were doing good. Official superiors would often be harsh to their inferiors, who would take it out on the travelling public. Under state socialism, there is no security whatever either that railway officials (except the highest) will have a tolerable life, or that railways will be run in the public interest.

In the case of railways, as in all analogous cases, there are two interests to be considered : (1) the interest of those who work on the railway ; (2) the interest of those who use the railway, especially for the carriage of goods. These have, of course, very little in common, so that any system which represents only one of them is inadequate. Roughly speaking, the co-operative movement tackles the question of modern industry from the point of view of the con- sumer, while trade unionism and syndicalism tackle it from the point of view of the producer. It is a mistake to say, as guild socialists did at first, that the State represents the consumer as against the producer. It is a geographical accident whether the State represents the producer or the consumer. Take the present House of Commons. The members for mining constituencies take essentially a producer's point of view ; so do most of the members for Lancashire constituencies. The members from the Clyde will take a producer's point of view of shipbuilding, but a consumer's point of view of rent. A State which erects a protective tariff takes a producer's point of view. *Cæteris paribus*, a Parliament will take a producer's point of view if there is much geographical concentration of industries, and a consumer's point of view if most constituencies are very mixed in their industrial composition. The State cannot, therefore, be regarded as essentially either on one side or on the other.

Neither the interests of the producer, nor those of the consumer, can be adequately represented except by *ad hoc* organizations. The producers are, of course, as a rule, much easier to organize, except for the fact that, so long as capitalism lasts, there is conflict between labour and capital in every branch of production. If capitalism were eliminated, the political strength of production as against consumption might be greatly increased. If so, the need of organizing consumers to protect their own interests would become much greater.

It is sometimes said that a man who is both a producer and a consumer, as most men are, will be actuated equally by the two interests, and will, therefore, have the necessary equilibrium within himself. This ignores the effect of organization. If a man belongs to an organization of all who share his interests as producer, but does not belong to any corresponding

consumers' organization, his wishes *qua* producer will
have political force, while his wishes *qua* consumer will
remain impotent. Wishes which in any way conflict
with those of some organized group must themselves
be organized if they are to have any chance of being
realized. Therefore, consumers' organizations are as
necessary as trade unions.

If both producers and consumers were organized,
it might be assumed that the State would be neutral
as between the two. It might, therefore be fairly
safe to leave the State to decide the issue when the
two kinds of organization came into conflict. The
officials of any large producing group, such as mines
or railways, would be primarily responsible to the
producers in that group, but would be subject to
expert criticism by the officials of the consumers'
organization, who might cause the State to revise the
decisions of the producers' officials in cases where the
public was adversely affected. This system may seem
somewhat elaborate, but where, as in an industrial
community, a portion of a man's interests are already
organized, this portion will win at the expense of the
whole unless the other portion also is organized. The
undue power of officials rests upon the fact that the
interest they represent is organized, while the interest
with which they conflict is often unorganized. Only
a more all-round organization can safeguard liberty
under these circumstances.

For the purpose of securing that the effective public
opinion shall be well-informed, it is very important
that vocational organizations should secure publicity
among their members by means of vocational journals.
The ordinary press has neither the will nor the space
to give accurate accounts of any issue that may arise.
So long as men rely upon ordinary newspapers, they

will be misled in the interests of one party or another. Vocational journals are, therefore a vital adjunct to vocational organizations.

As to the means by which organizations of producers and consumers are to acquire power, the obvious means are the strike and the boycott. As a rule, the mere possibility of employing these methods is sufficient, but it is essential, at any rate until we have a better economic system, that no legal obstacle should exist to their actual employment when methods of negotiation fail. At present, both methods are everywhere legal for capitalists, and the strike is legal for labour in this country. In various other countries, though technically legal, it can generally be made to involve some indirect infringement of the law. America, in particular, has developed the method of the injunction into a fine art.

If the struggle against capitalism were successfully disposed of, it might be possible to introduce certain safeguards to minimize the use of the strike and the boycott. It might be possible for the State to demand that every dispute should first be submitted to its arbitrament, and to side against any disputant refusing this demand. There must still be the legal possibility of a strike, since the State is not unlikely to treat minorities unjustly ; but at any rate for the guidance of public opinion the judicial decision of the State should be given before a strike actually takes place.

We may sum up what has been said in this chapter and its predecessor as follows : Undue power arises where one set of interests is better organized than another set with which the first conflicts. Under these circumstances, justice and liberty can only be secured by better organization of the weaker interests. This applies to military power in the sphere of international politics ; to economic power in the sphere of industry and finance ; and to the power of the bureaucracy in the State and in big business organizations. Rights will never be respected unless they have power to make themselves respected, but this power can always be won by organization and energy. The result may be for a time a tug of war of rival interests, but in the end people will come to rely upon negotiation, all the more readily when no more favourable result is to be expected from more violent methods, which will be the case when all the interests concerned are duly represented in the negotiations by appropriate organizations. This method may not be ideal, but it seems the best that is possible in our imperfect world.

CHAPTER XII

EDUCATION

THE subject of education is one of the most difficult that any reformer has to consider. It might seem at first sight as though education afforded the key to social improvement, since undoubtedly better education would make all other reforms easy. But in fact most of the evils of existing education are direct consequences of the other evils from which industrial civilization is suffering, and cannot be radically cured until our economic system has been changed. Nevertheless something can be done, through public opinion among teachers, and to a lesser extent among parents, to make education less harmful in the meantime. There is not any one key position to be captured by those who aim at a less competitive and unjust organization of society; there are a number of connected positions to be attacked simultaneously, since any advance in one place brings with it correlated advances in all the others. In this chapter, we are concerned, not with education in Utopia, but with what can be done here and now to prevent the grosser evils of education as it is at present. I propose to confine myself in the main to elementary education, since that alone can be considered as one of those mass phenomena with which this book is concerned.

Our central problem in this book has been to inquire

242

how far it is possible to combine the uniformity and large-scale organization which industrialism demands on the material side with diversity, individuality and spontaneity in the non-material aspects of life. This problem takes on its most acute form in connection with education : is it inevitable that education, in an industrial community, should have the characteristic defects of machine-made products ? Or is it possible to have machinery in industry without having a mechanistic outlook in our thoughts and in the mental habits which our education forces upon the young ?

Elementary education, at present, is conducted mainly by the State, and to a smaller extent by the Churches with the help of the State. Both systems have defects, but not the same defects. State education has the vices characteristic of the modern world : nationalism, glorification of competition and success, worship of mechanism, love of uniformity and contempt for individuality. The teaching of the churches is equally nationalistic, but in other respects it is mediæval rather than modern. It aims at producing submission to authority, belief in nonsense through the hypnotic effect of early and frequent repetition, respect for superior individuals rather than for the spirit of the herd. It is difficult to say whether the State or the Church does the greater damage to the minds and hearts of children.

If there is to be universal compulsory education, it is practically unavoidable that it should be financed by the State. Within this necessity there are, however, two possibilities : the State may also administer education, or it may leave the administration to private organizations, confining itself to inspection to ensure efficient instruction. *A priori*, the latter might seem the better method, since it is likely to secure greater diversity, and enable parents to find schools suited to their tastes. If there were no churches, this argument would have more weight than it has ; but in practice, the only organizations which will take the trouble to provide education on a large scale are the Churches, and they do so in order to prevent children from thinking, since they know that most people who think do not accept any particular brand of orthodoxy. Although I am conscious of rashness in advancing such an opinion, I doubt whether an education designed to prevent thought is the best possible. Therefore, the advantages of an education conducted by organizations other than the State must be admitted to be problematical in the present state of opinion.

There are, however, some further arguments in favour of education by organizations other than the State. At present, the State is not impartial as regards the bodies to which it will delegate education. It admits Roman Catholics and Anglicans, whose schools it is willing to finance, but it would not admit socialists. If the Independent Labour Party were to start elementary schools, it is not to be supposed that the present State would treat them as kindly as it treats traditional religions.[1] This, however, might be remedied at no very distant date, and, if so, many working-class children might receive an education free from capitalist bias. This is a matter which might profitably absorb some of the thoughts of the first Labour Government, when it comes.

[1] *The Times*, in a telegram dated "Melbourne, February 20, 1923," states : "The New South Wales Minister of Justice is alarmed at the existence in Sydney of Communist Sunday Schools, in which subversive propaganda prevails. In a Bill which he proposes to introduce in the State Parliament he intends to provide for three months' imprisonment with a fine of £50 for any one who teaches children under 15 years seditious or anarchical doctrines." Conservative M.P.s are urging similar legislation here (*The Times*, February 27, 1923).

In the second place, the existing State, just as much as the Churches, is based upon superstitions which are only genuinely believed by thoughtless or interested persons. Nationalism, capitalism and reverence for the authorities are superstitions which form an essential part of State education, and undoubtedly they are very harmful superstitions. The best that can be said for them, as compared with Church dogmas, is that, to most minds, they are not so difficult to believe, and that they do not cover so large a part of the world of thought. They can therefore be instilled with less artificiality, and with less isolation from vigorous contemporary opinion, than a religious education demands. But this advantage is temporary. The more the State feels itself menaced, the more it has to shield its school children from contact with modern ideas, and the more it has to devote itself to producing artificial stupidity. The superiority of the State to the Church hitherto has arisen from the fact that it was less challenged. As this ceases to be a fact, the State will become just as obscurantist as the Church.

But whatever may be thought of the merits or demerits of the State, it is highly probable that most of the education will be in the hands of the State for a long time to come. The question of practical interest is : can any force be brought to bear to mitigate the evils of State education ?

Not much reliance can be placed on the public opinion of parents. Parents, in the main, want their children taught whatever is necessary for earning a living, and if they are religious, they want them taught religion ; but they do not as a rule care what kind of outlook the children acquire, so long as it is not conventionally shocking, and the great majority of parents are not sufficiently educated to realize how mechanical and dry most of the instruction is.

The best hope is with the teachers. What the teachers could insist upon is complete freedom so long as the actual instruction is satisfactory. That is to say, they could demand, and secure, that a teacher in a State school shall not suffer by reason of his opinions, or the opinions which he expresses in teaching, or his activities outside school hours, so long as there is no fault to be found with the actual knowledge of his pupils. A peculiarly gross case of interference with the liberty of the teacher has been taking place on a large scale in most parts of England lately ; I mean the dismissal of married women teachers.[1] It is not pretended that a married woman is a worse teacher than an unmarried one. In fact, everyone knows that celibate women, when they are no longer quite young, are liable to hysteria and faults of temper which make them less desirable as teachers than women who have led a more natural life. But of course no education authority cares about education.

An even more serious interference with the liberty of the teacher has been enforced during the last few years in the State of New York.[2] In that State, no school, not even one wholly supported by private funds, is allowed to exist if " it shall appear that the instruction proposed to be given includes the teachings of the doctrine that organized governments shall be overthrown by force, violence, or unlawful means." In State schools, no person is by law allowed to teach unless he is " loyal and obedient to the Government of this State and of the United States,"

[1] For an account of a vigorous Labour protest against this policy, see *Daily Herald*, March 3, 1923.

[2] See *The New Republic*, February 1, 1922.

or if he has ever advocated "a form of Government other than the Government of this State or of the United States." The Lusk Committee, to which these laws are due, laid it down that a teacher who does not approve of the present social system must surrender his office, and that all teachers must be "eager to combat the theories of social change." This is the same policy that has been pursued by the Bolsheviks since they acquired power.[1] It is the policy which will be pursued by any State when it feels its existence in danger, provided the teachers are willing to submit. It means that no person who has either a heart or a brain can be a school teacher, unless he is so pusillanimous as to be willing to keep his opinions to himself.

This state of affairs could be remedied by the efforts of the teachers, if they had an adequate conception of the dignity of their profession, and a determination not to be hampered in the performance of their proper

[1] For an official exposition of Bolshevik educational policy, see three articles by Lunatcharsky on popular education in the *Communist International* for 1919. The policy of some, at least, of the British dominions is just as bad as that of New York State. "The *Maoriland Worker* has been summoned to answer a charge of blasphemous libel for publishing a poem by Siegfried Sassoon, 'Stand-to: Good Friday Morning.' Noah Ablett's *Outlines of Economics* and Friedrich Engels' *Socialism, Utopian and Scientific* have been added to the list of books which are not allowed to come into the country. Teachers, and even University professors and lecturers of the Workers' Educational Association (which is subject to a measure of government control) must give up the right to think for themselves or lose their jobs. A W.E.A. lecturer was recently dismissed on the ground of alleged Bolshevik views. Another, whose subject is Maori lore, will not be reappointed owing to his connection with the Communist Party, and that though there is not the slightest evidence that his lectures contained any reference whatever to Communism. Miss Weitzel, a brilliant student, 20 years of age, was fined for selling the *Communist*, and dismissed from the Training College. Prevented by the immigration laws of the United States from joining her German parents in that country, she is now trying to earn her living as a housemaid-waitress" (*Daily Herald*, January 14, 1922).

function. The National Union of Teachers is a very strong body, and could be even stronger if it made itself the champion of the best educational ideals. It should insist that no teacher should be dismissed except for educational incompetence, i.e. failure to give the requisite instruction. When any case of dismissal on this ground occurs, the National Union of Teachers should itself inquire into the circumstances, and satisfy itself that the ground alleged is the *bona fide* ground, not a cloak for some unavowed enmity. When this point had been won, it should endeavour to secure gradually increasing freedom for head-masters from the regulations of the Board of Education or the local Education Authority, subject always to the maintenance of a high level in instruction. The head-master should have freedom in the choice of text-books, and some degree of freedom as to the curriculum in the higher standards. All this would, of course, be inconvenient for the authorities, but it is not wise to sacrifice education for the convenience of officials.

There should be no insistence that the teacher should preserve what is called "impartiality," i.e. should express only those opinions which are held by the majority of the Education Authority. The best teachers are not impartial; they are men of strong enthusiasms, to which they wish to give expression in their teaching. The impartiality of the learner is best secured by exposing him to teachers with opposite prejudices, not by giving him only such teaching as will seem colourless to men who think that the truth must be what is commonly believed. If the result is scepticism as to all violent opinions, so much the better; that is the very attitude of mind that the modern world most needs in the mass of mankind.

In the course of imparting instruction, a teacher inevitably has certain effects upon the character and aptitudes of his pupils. If teachers are themselves fired by certain ideals of life, they will communicate these ideals to a certain percentage of their pupils. I am not thinking of definite propaganda, for Catholicism or Socialism or any other " ism." Of such propaganda there is already far too much, especially in education. I am thinking of less definite things : intellectual honesty, tolerance, broad-mindedness, love of knowledge—the things that constitute what one may call the intellectual virtues. A boy will naturally like whatever seems to support the side to which he belongs : a Manchester boy will be impatient when he hears praise of Liverpool, and *vice versa*. But boys can be taught to like fairness in thought, just as they can be taught to like fairness in games. It is a pity that the spirit of fair play is thought wicked when applied in the intellectual sphere ; for example, the man who denies falsehoods about the enemy in war time is regarded as a traitor.

Definite opinions in a teacher may often rouse opposition in pupils, but ideals in which he genuinely believes are likely to have considerable influence. What should be the ideals that a teacher sets before himself ?

There are two aims which an educational system may endeavour to realize : to make good citizens, or to make good human beings. Conceived broadly and philosophically, these two aims do not conflict ; but conceived narrowly, as administrators are likely to conceive them, they conflict very seriously. The man who is imbued with the mechanistic outlook will try to make good citizens rather than good men, and will conceive good citizenship in a way which almost excludes good humanity. In the notion of good citizenship as conceived by governments I see three disastrous errors :

First, each man or woman is conceived as the citizen of a single State, not of the world ;

Secondly, the State or the community is supposed to have a good other and higher than that of its several citizens ;

Thirdly, the good is conceived as something which can be realized by purely mechanical means, not as something dependent upon the mental quality of individuals.

The first of these errors, namely, nationalism, has no intrinsic connection with mechanism, but has been enormously strengthened by the way in which industrialism has been developed nationally, so that the connection with machinery is very close in fact, if not in logic.

Of course the basis of any public educational system must be the imparting of that necessary minimum of knowledge without which a man cannot play his part in a modern community. It is necessary that everybody should be able to read and write, add up a column of figures, and so on. As time goes on, the State increases the minimum of knowledge, which may come gradually to be quite considerable. But I am not concerned to discuss this basis, important as it is, since it may be taken as agreed. I am concerned rather to discuss those things as to which disagreement is possible.

In the course of instruction, the schoolmaster has the opportunity to instil certain mental habits. It is here that disagreement begins : what mental habits shall he teach ? There are all sorts of possibilities. Jesuits, in the process of giving admirable instruction, taught their pupils to accept unquestioningly the dogmas of the Catholic Church. American elementary schools teach the children to become 100 per cent. Americans, i.e. to believe that America is God's own country, its constitution divinely inspired, and its millionaires models of Sunday-school virtue. English elementary schools teach that our Empire is great and beneficent, that it has never oppressed India or forced opium on China, that it has been invariably humanitarian in Africa, and that all Germans are wicked. Russian elementary schools teach that Communists are virtuous, anarchists wicked, and the bourgeois misguided; that the social revolution is imminent throughout Europe; and that there cannot be any imperialism in the Communist Party because all imperialism is due to capitalism. The Japanese teach that the Mikado is a divine being, descended from the sun goddess; that Japan was created earlier than other parts of the earth; and that it is therefore the duty of the Chinese to submit meekly to whatever commands the Japanese may lay upon them. I understand that similar doctrines are taught in Uruguay, Paraguay, and San Marino, each of which is specially favoured by Heaven, and vastly more virtuous than its neighbours. In short, wherever a sovereign government exists, it uses its monopoly of the teaching of writing and reading to force upon the young a set of ridiculous beliefs of which the purpose is to increase their willingness to commit homicide.[1] And for the sake of these beliefs, mental

---

[1] A reading-book adopted by the French Board of Education for use in Alsace-Lorraine says : " Do not forget ! bear it in mind, little Frenchmen, that it was Germany which attacked France and forced the Great War upon her. . . . The Germans committed ghastly crimes : they mutilated and killed the children, they shot down women and the aged. . . . Eternal shame upon Germany ! Eternal glory to gracious France and her Allies " (*Daily Herald*, May 15, 1922).

habits of a peculiar kind are also encouraged : credulity, blind prejudice, and group ferocity—all of them characteristics natural to primitive man, which education might have been expected to soften.

The governors of the world believe, and have always believed, that virtue can only be taught by teaching falsehood, and that any man who knew the truth would be wicked. I disbelieve this, absolutely and entirely. I believe that love of truth is the basis of all real virtue, and that virtues based upon lies can only do harm. Perhaps I should in any case believe this as an article of faith, but in fact there is abundant evidence of it. The case of nationalism is admirable as an illustration. The text-books out of which history is taught are known by every education minister in the world to be deliberately and intentionally misleading owing to patriotic bias. It is not merely that the history taught is false ; the really bad thing is that its falsehood is of a sort to make wars more likely. Much is said by socialists, very justly, about the importance of internationalism in the economic sphere ; but internationalism in the educational sphere is at least as important. If children in all civilized countries were taught the same history, different countries would hate each other less, and no country would feel so confident of victory in an appeal to arms. Text-books ought to be drawn up by an international authority, which should direct the training of historical teachers. The present practice increases each nation's belief in its own righteousness and power, and, therefore, its willingness to go to war. Indeed, this appears to be the reason for which the present mendacious teaching exists.

So great is this evil that it may well be found, in

the end, to outweigh all the good that is done by
instruction. The illiterate peasant in Russia or China
is not a nationalist, because he cannot realize anything
so large and abstract as his nation ; when his country
is at war, he regards it as an affair of the government,
in which his part is limited to reluctantly obeying
orders. This is the reason why Russia and China
cannot do as much harm to other countries as is done
by England or France, or was done by Germany.
If Russia and China develop elementary education
on the lines which Western nations have made familiar,
they will be able to rely upon their vast populations
for the degree of patriotic blindness which made the
late war possible ; and when that happens the little
nations of Western Europe will be sorry that, like
Macbeth, they taught

> Bloody instructions, which, being taught, return
> To plague the inventor.

All the accumulation of horror which lies before us
through the growing virulence of nationalism would
be prevented if education aimed at teaching facts
instead of fictions, or if education authorities could
conceive of boys and girls as future citizens of the
world, not only of the particular geographical area in
which they happen to live.

It would, of course, be unfair to put down the whole
pugnacious nationalism of our time to faulty education.
Loyalty to one's group, pride in its achievements
(real or imaginary), and hostility to rival groups,
are all part of the instinctive apparatus in man. All
that has been done by education is to appeal to this
instinct, and to direct it into a certain channel. The
men who direct education are themselves subject
to it, and do not consciously or deliberately go against

what they believe to be right. It is quite possible that, when they realize the imminent collapse of Western civilization as a result of their yielding to instinct, they may come to understand that, in this respect as in many others, education ought to aim at the control of crude instinct by a rational prevision of consequences, and at the training of instinctive passions so as to help rather than hinder the life of the world. At present, in private life, very few of us are murderers, though in a savage community of head-hunters most men are. In such communities, everything is done to strengthen the instinct towards private homicide, which among ourselves is successfully repressed except in unusually violent people. But as regards public homicide, in war, the line taken among ourselves is exactly analogous to that which head-hunters take as regards private homicide. The methods which have enabled us to overcome the instinct of private murder would enable us to overcome the same instinct when it takes the form of love of war. Such methods ought to be used in education, instead of the present methods, which nourish the little seed of instinct until it grows into the vast tree of national armaments and international suspicions.

The feeling that mankind are all one family, and that the division into nations is a trivial folly, could very easily be produced in the average boy or girl if education were directed to that end. A book like Wells's *Outline of History*, which begins with the geological and biological antecedents of the human species, and treats human progress always as a single movement to which many nations have contributed, is likely to produce a far broader and more humane outlook than chauvinistic teaching about Agincourt and Trafalgar, or Lexington and Saratoga. Perhaps it may be necessary to the due exercise of all our instincts to have *some* object of hatred. In the Middle Ages, the Devil could be hated without harm to human beings ; but in our time few people have any vivid belief in his existence, in spite of the war and the peace. We must, therefore, find some other non-human object of hatred, if men are to be prevented from hating their neighbours in other countries. One might hate matter, like the Manichæans, or ignorance, or disease. To hate these things would do good ; and by a little symbolism it could be made to satisfy our instinctive craving for hatred. But to hate other groups of human beings can only do harm, and it is monstrous that education should aim at instilling such hatred by means of lies and suppressions. Yet such is the case in every one of the great nations, except China, which is bullied and despised in consequence.

I come now to the second error which, as I think, mechanism has encouraged in our education : the error of imagining that the State, or the community as a whole, is capable of some different kind of good from that which exists in individuals, and that this collective good is somehow higher than that which is realized in individuals. This belief constitutes what I should propose to call the "administrator's fallacy." It is, of course, by no means a fallacy to suppose that an individual can only enjoy the best life when he lives in a community having certain qualities ; I do not suggest that Robinson Crusoe could have as good an existence as (say) an Athenian citizen in the age of Pericles. (Perhaps the age of Pericles was really no better than our own, but it is correct to suppose that it was good, and I accept the supposition for the sake of illustration.) The fallacy that I am attacking is not the obvious truism that certain kinds of communities are a means to good things in the lives of their citizens, but the quite different proposition that, when account has been taken of all the good things in individual lives, there remains something good or bad belonging to the State or community as a personified entity. This doctrine was preached by Hegel, and adopted by his British disciples. It has an elaborate logical foundation, which I believe to be wholly erroneous, for reasons which I have often set forth. On the present occasion, it is its consequences, not its premisses, that I wish to examine.

Those who accept this theory of the peculiar value attaching to States or communities as such call their theory the " organic " view of society. This name is somewhat misleading, for it is of course evident that a society is more or less organic, in the sense that it has interrelated parts which minister to common ends, as the parts of an animal's body minister to the life of the whole. The obviousness of this fact makes people willing to accept without much scrutiny a view which says that it is only asserting the organic nature of society. But, in fact, the sociologists in question use the word " organic " in a peculiar philosophical sense of their own. They mean that a society is a single entity with a life of its own, not merely a number of more or less co-operating interrelated persons. They would argue that a person enjoys good things which belong neither to his head nor to his arms nor to his great toe, but to him as a single whole, and that, in like manner, the State enjoys good things which are not to be found in the lives of single citizens. And they generally contend also that the highest function of the citizens is to minister to the life of the State, just as the highest function of the various organs of a man's body is to minister to the life of the man.

Thus our duty to the State becomes something more imperative than our duty to our neighbour, and the good of the State might conceivably have to be pursued by measures involving injury to the great majority of its citizens.

In practice, this view leads to the advocacy of an aristocratic and mechanical society. "The good of the State," is, in practice, "the good of the statesman." I do not mean this in a crude sense ; by "the good of the statesman," I do not mean merely his wealth, or any of the things which conventionally constitute the aims of self-interested people. These things may, of course, be involved, but a high-minded man will be on his guard against them. There are other subtler forms of selfishness against which men are much less on their guard, and to which they are likely to succumb unconsciously. A man who is in the habit of thinking about the State finds pleasure in contemplating a certain kind of State, and almost inevitably falls into the habit of thinking that this kind of State is good. A man of administrative temperament finds pleasure in contemplating a State where there is a great deal of administration, where there is a tidy system, and every person has his place as a cog in the machinery. Such a State will be intolerable to men of a different temperament, for instance, to artists. But such men, just because of their temperament, will not become politicians or civil servants or captains of industry. Thus one kind of temperament, and that not a very common one, is, in practice, alone concerned in establishing what it considers "the good of the State." This kind of temperament, so long as "the good of the State " is believed in, will feel free to force its tastes upon the community, since they are supposed to be the tastes of the personified State. This means a

17

persecution of decent people by busybodies, and a gradual crushing-out of art and thought and simple enjoyment of life.

Men who advocate what they call the "organic" view of the State always imagine that what they believe in is an antithesis to mechanism. This is a most curious delusion. A machine is essentially organic, in the sense that it has parts which co-operate to produce a single useful result, and that the separate parts have little value on their own account. A machine may not be so perfect an example of an organism as an animal is, but we can make machines and we cannot make animals. Therefore when we are exhorted to make society "organic," it is from machinery that we shall necessarily derive our imaginative models, since we do not know how to make society a living animal. Moreover, nothing has done so much to make communities organic as the introduction of mechanical industrial processes, which have necessitated the co-operation of vast organizations in great enterprises such as railways, and have made men, through the need of commerce, far more dependent upon other men than they were in simpler times. Thus mechanism, in the concrete form of machinery, ministers to belief in "the good of the State," and in turn dictates the form which that belief is to take ; the good of the State consists in having as much machinery as possible, regardless of what it produces, whether useful commodities or poison gases.

It is interesting to observe that the Bolsheviks, who, as disciples of Marx, have retained what Marx retained of Hegel's teaching, are among the most ardent believers in the good of the State as opposed to the good of the citizens. Their aim—I speak of those who are public-spirited and not self-seeking—

is to produce a certain type of society which they
believe to be good in itself, quite regardless of the
question whether it will bring happiness to those who
have to live in it. One cannot but observe (though
they themselves are unconscious of the fact) that the
society they aim at would bring happiness to vigorous
administrators having a good position in the official
hierarchy, and probably to no one else. Similarly
the Kaiser and the Junkers sought the good of
" Germany " as opposed to the good of Germans ;
but it happened that the good of " Germany," as they
conceived it, coincided with that of the Kaiser and
the Junkers. And to come nearer home, those who
glory in the British Empire are willing that for its
sake all its citizens should suffer—excepting, of course,
those who govern it, who will have the pleasure of
contemplating the sort of Empire that suits their
tastes. One might say the same of the industrial and
financial magnates in America, and of governing
persons generally. All such persons, unless they are
very much on their guard against the administrator's
fallacy, will have a conception of the public good which
is unconsciously biassed so as to secure their own
good.

It is not merely the injustice of this view that
constitutes its harmfulness, it is still more (which was
my third point) the second-rate and mechanical
quality of the goods valued by the ordinary administrative temperament. The great artists, the great
thinkers, and the great religious teachers of the world
have had quite other standards ; they have valued the
individual, they have praised spontaneous impulse,
they have conceived the good life as one lived from
within, not forced into conformity to an external
mechanism. They have not sought to make men

convenient material for the manipulations of rulers, but to make them spiritually free to pursue what they believed to be good, regardless of law and public opinion. This was the teaching of Christ, of Buddha, of Lao-Tze ; in another form, the same emphasis on the individual is to be found in Shakespeare, and in Galileo's resistance to the Inquisition. All that is best in human life depends upon a certain kind of self-respect, self-determination ; a man who has allowed outside pressure to dictate the ends for which he shall live can never be more than a slave.

Our modern State education is mainly designed to produce convenient citizens, and therefore dare not encourage spontaneity, since all spontaneity interferes with system. There is a tendency to uniformity, to the suppression of private judgment, to the production of populations which are tame towards their rulers and ferocious towards "the enemy." Even if our civilization escapes destruction in great wars, this tendency of State education to produce mental slavery will, if it is not checked, kill out everything of value in the way of art and thought, and even ultimately of human affection, and it inevitably kills the joy of life, which cannot exist where spontaneity is dead.

It must not be supposed that democracy, by itself, offers any cure for these evils, which come from the intensity of government, and are independent of its form. Wherever there is great intensity of government, effective power is in the hands of officials, and the bias of officials (apart from rare exceptions) is always towards mechanism. A majority may be quite as oppressive as a minority ; and the champions of any new good thing will hardly ever be a majority. Room for individual initiative, absence of uniformity, are essential conditions of progress ; the tyranny which threatens us in the future is not so much that of any privileged class as that of the energetic people who like politics and administration. Formerly, the power of such people was very limited; now, owing to industrialism and the consequent increased destructiveness of wars, the power of the State is enormously greater than ever before in the history of mankind. If there were only one world-wide State, the danger would still exist, but would be easier to combat. Owing, however, to the existence of many States, the main purpose of every great State is success in war, and it is to this end that the immense power of the State is mainly devoted. This end is not served by the preservation of individual initiative, and thus the tendencies to a mechanical enslavement of ordinary men and women are enormously strengthened by the need of preparing for war. It is impossible to exaggerate the harmful influence of these tendencies upon education in all the leading countries of the world.

It may be thought that I have strayed rather far from the subject of education in the course of these remarks. But a system of education embodies the ideals of the society which establishes it, and cannot be radically reformed except by a reform of ideals. If I had to direct the training of teachers, there are two things that I should specially impress upon them :

First, that a man's public duty is towards mankind as a whole, not towards any subordinate group such as a nation or a class ;

Secondly, that a good community is a community of good men and women—of men and women, that is to say, who live freely but not destructively or oppressively.

As to the first point, I should try to bring about a

realization of the disaster which faces our civilization if science invents continually new means of destruction without being counteracted by a simultaneous ethical advance. Many people see the danger, but few are willing to dissociate themselves from the governmental and popular forces which are making for new wars, and few are willing to face the fact that patriotism, in its common form, is the worst vice of which a modern man can be guilty. To bring a realization of these things should be part of the business of every educator ; he should try to teach impartiality of judgment, the habit of searching for impersonal truth, and distrust of party catchwords. He should try also to counteract the natural tendency to believe that men belonging to opposing groups or nations are specially wicked. Under the influence of skilful propaganda, our impulse to moral indignation is exploited to make us hate those whom our masters wish us to hate ; and under the influence of the resulting hatred, we do things which rouse the moral indignation of those whom we hate. Thus moral indignation has become a source of evil in the world. Punishment is seldom the best way to deal with men's imperfections, and there is hardly any-one so blameless as to have a right to administer it. As things stand, we know the sins of our enemies, but not our own sins ; thus indignation produces merely an increase of mutual enmity. Americans, for example, know the atrocities of which Japan has been guilty in Korea, which are unknown to nine Japanese out of ten ; Japanese, on the other hand, know the worst that is to be said about the lynching of negroes in America far better than Americans do. Thus hatred is stimulated on both sides, and nothing is done on either side to check the evils. Indignation against the criminal is seldom useful ; what is useful is compassion for the victim, and willingness to face the fact that it is not only our enemies who make victims. I think, however, that in education it would be more useful to dwell upon the interconnection of different parts of the world than upon what may be called humanitarian arguments. It is easy to see and to teach that we cannot ruin our enemies without ruining ourselves, and that, from mere self-preservation, enmities between nations cannot continue if the world is to maintain its present population.

As to the second point—the freedom of the individual —this is quite peculiarly matter for the educator, because the freedom that we can hope to preserve is rather mental and spiritual than economic or material. Industrialism has made it necessary that, in what concerns the material side of life, men should co-operate in vast organizations. It is just that the community should exact from every able-bodied adult an amount of productive work corresponding to what he or she consumes. It seems inevitable that, as regards this necessary minimum of labour, there shall be less freedom in future than has been enjoyed hitherto by the fortunate minority. But if we could abolish wars and armaments and advertisement and the waste of commercial competition, we could all subsist comfortably on about four hours' work a day. The rest of our time ought to be free, and education ought to prepare us for an intelligent use of the twenty hours a day during which we should be left to our own initiative. In the future, as in the past, whatever form of socialism or communism may be instituted, we must expect that all the best work will be done voluntarily, without reward, owing to an impulse from within. Given equal opportunity for all, we may hope that there will be much more of such work than there has hitherto been. But there will be none at all if the State, in its schools, sets to work to mould the minds of the young according to a uniform plan. There must be the utmost encouragement to freedom of thought, even when it is inconvenient to bureaucrats. There must be opportunities for voluntary teachers—especially after childhood is past—who will teach because they wish to do so, and not merely for a livelihood. In everything that lies outside the provision of the necessaries of life, there must be individualism, personal initiative, variety. The fight for freedom is not to be won by any mere change in our economic system. It is to be won only by a constant resistance to the tyranny of officials, and a constant realization that mental freedom is the most precious of all goods. Mechanism has its place : its place is in the material side of life, the provision of the food and clothes and houses without which we cannot live. But it has no place in what makes life worth preserving, in art and thought, in friendship and love, or in simple enjoyment. These things demand freedom—not only outward freedom, but freedom in our minds and hearts. Such freedom is too little respected in our schools and in the schemes of economic reformers. It is in danger of being lost through the tyranny of purely material aims. But no perfection of organization can ever compensate for its loss : and nothing can prevent its loss unless we remember that man cannot live by bread alone.

CHAPTER XIII

ECONOMIC ORGANIZATION AND MENTAL FREEDOM

IN the first part of this book, we saw that machinery, which is physically capable of conferring great benefits upon mankind, is instead inflicting untold evil, of which the worst may be still to come. We traced this evil to three sources : private property, nationalism, and the mechanistic outlook. We found that if mechanism is to become a boon to mankind, private property, at least as regards land and all natural and legal monopolies, must be replaced by some form of public ownership and control ; nationalism must give place to internationalism, both as regards sentiment and as regards certain governmental functions, notably war, movements of population, and the distribution of raw materials ; while the mechanistic outlook must give place to one which values mechanism for its extra-mechanical uses, but no longer worships it as a good in itself. We found that there is not, as Marxians contend, something fatal about sociological development, but that, on the contrary, it can be controlled and completely changed by public opinion and the operation of human desires and beliefs. This becomes more and more true as men advance in intelligence and in control over nature. We are at this moment the victims, not of natural forces outside ourselves, but of our own folly and our own evil passions. " The fault, dear Brutus, is not in our stars, but in ourselves." It is popular philosophy that is at fault ; if that were changed, all the evils in the world would melt away.

In this final chapter, I wish first to set forth the distinction between the mechanistic outlook and the humanistic outlook which is its opposite ; then to show how, if the evil effects of the mechanistic outlook were overcome, it would be possible to use machinery for the liberation of life, not for its enslavement to a dance of death.

The distinction between the mechanistic and the humanistic conceptions of excellence is the most fundamental of all distinctions between rival sets of ideals. The mechanistic conception regards the good as something outside the individual, as something which is realized through a society as a whole, whether voluntarily co-operating or not. The humanistic conception, on the other hand, regards the good as something existing in the lives of individuals, and conceives social co-operation as only valuable in so far as it ministers to the welfare of the several citizens. The mechanistic conception is not interested in the individual as such, but only in the part that he can play as a cog in the machinery. It will endeavour so to train and alter his nature as to make him sub-missive when the Plan of the Whole thwarts his individual desires. He must be taught to say to the State : "Thy will be done." On the other hand the humanistic conception regards a child as a gardener regards a young tree, i.e. as something with a certain intrinsic nature, which will develop into an admirable form given proper soil and air and light. The extreme of the mechanistic view is Calvinism ; the extreme of the humanistic view is Taoism.

The Calvinist conceives human beings as existing, not for their own sakes, but for the glory of God ; those who are saved minister to His glory, since they afford occasion for the Divine mercy ; those who are damned minister equally to His glory, since they afford occasion for the Divine justice. It does not signify, therefore, whether many are saved and few damned, or many damned and few saved : either result is equally admirable. Calvinists held that few were saved, though it usually happened—by a pure accident—that they themselves were among the elect. Men were saved by predestination, not by merit ; their salvation or damnation was quite independent of whether they led virtuous or sinful lives. Taking account of the fact that the immense majority of mankind were damned eternally, human life, here and hereafter, afforded an immense balance of misery and wickedness (for the damned remain always wicked) ; yet that was no ground for regretting the creation of human beings, since they contributed to the glory of God, which alone was important.

The Calvinist outlook is supposed to be nearly extinct, and people think that they see its absurdities. But to my mind the present mechanistic outlook, particularly as it exists among the great capitalists, is almost indistinguishable from Calvinism. Put the machine in place of God, the efficiency of the machine in place of the glory of God, the rich and the poor in place of the saved and the damned, inheritance in place of predestination ; you will then find that every tenet of Calvinism has its counterpart in the modern religion of industrialism. According to this religion, men exist, not in order that they may be happy, but in order that machines may be prolific. I have heard men engaged in the development of Africa complain that the great obstacle was the happiness of the natives, who were able to live without work ; to cure this, governments of white men impose a hut tax, which cannot be paid unless the native agrees to work for a white exploiter. The white men who act in this way are not actuated by mere self-interest ; they are actuated by religion, just as truly as the mediæval inquisitor. Again, our system produces a few rich and many poor, but is not to be condemned on that account, if it could not be changed without detracting from the glory of the machine. Who is to be rich is settled, in most cases, by inheritance, not by merit, just as God's unmotived free choice predestined certain people to be among the elect and the rest to be among the reprobate. Both religions agree in placing the purpose of human life outside human life itself, and from this source flows the cruelty which both have in common.

Human nature has many curious perversities, and one of the most curious is this : that we tend to worship whatever is useful to us, and, by worshipping it, to deprive it of its utility. Men worshipped agriculture, and propitiated the god of vegetation by human sacrifice ; what this meant in cruelty and horror may be seen, for instance, in Prescott's " Conquest of Mexico " interpreted in the light of Frazer's " Golden Bough." Men worshipped sex, and became sunk in phallic orgies ; by reaction, they worshipped chastity, and condemned themselves to life-long celibacy. The Australian aborigines, who are free from war and most of the evils that afflict other men, impose upon themselves exquisitely painful surgical operations, which greatly diminish their fertility ; they do this from a superstitious reverence for sex. In like manner the white races, having discovered machinery and realized its immense power, have allowed themselves to worship it, and have thereby made it maleficent. Until they cease to view it with awe, they will not be able to make it subserve the true ends of life.

In objecting to the mechanistic outlook, I am not objecting to machinery ; it is the *worship* of machinery, not the use of it, that does the harm. Agriculture still survives, though we have abandoned the worship of the corn spirit, with all its attendant horrors. Similarly the use of machines will survive, even if we cease to worship the god from the machine.

The extreme antithesis to the mechanistic outlook is the outlook of Taoism, which originated in China in the sixth century B.C. Taoism considers that everything, animate and inanimate, has a certain intrinsic nature, and that what is good is that everything should function according to its nature. This will happen if there is no outside interference. Chuang Tze, the St. Paul of Taoism, objects to every attempt to divert people or things from their natural course. He objects, of course, to government, since it consists in controlling people ; he objects to the Confucian maxim that we ought to love our neighbours, because we cannot do them any good, and our whole duty to them is to let them alone. He objects to roads and boats, to the domestication of horses, even to the arts of the potter and the carpenter, because all these are interferences with nature. A quotation [1] will illustrate his point of view :

The people have certain natural instincts—to weave and clothe themselves, to till and feed themselves. These are common to all humanity, and all are agreed thereon. Such instincts are called " Heaven-sent."

[1] Lionel Giles, *Musings of a Chinese Mystic*, pp. 67–8. For Legge's translation, see *Sacred Books of the East*, vol. xxxix. p. 277 ff. (Clarendon Press.)

as for wage-earners, a different social system would bring greater freedom, though it would probably not bring an increase in their material comforts.

The true function of industrialism, in a well-ordered community, is the provision of the necessaries of life, and of such comforts as can become widespread without entailing too much labour. If the labour of the community were directed by those who do the work, they would strike a balance between goods and leisure, which is now wholly lacking. The nation might decide to work an extra hour a day and enjoy more superfluities, or to work an hour less and have fewer goods with more spare time. There would be a strong incentive to the avoidance of useless labour. Under socialism, there would not be the spur of competition and profit to speed up industry. We should be saved the waste involved in advertisement, excessive plant, and marketing. If internationalism also were established, we should save the waste involved in armaments, international competition, diplomacy and customs. The result would be that the part of a man's life to be given to the community in the shape of necessary work would be very much less than at present, and the part in which he could follow his own devices would be much greater.

All this would require immense organization and the utilization of the best mechanical contrivances. It is not to be supposed that the compulsory work which a man would have to do for his living could, as a rule, be other than tedious and monotonous. Machine-minding cannot easily be humanized. But it would be possible to reduce compulsory work to a rather small amount. Probably with our present technique it could be reduced to four hours a day, and with every technical advance the amount could be diminished.

This, of course, assumes that it would be possible to avoid such an increase of population as to cause difficulties with the food supply. Socialism, especially international socialism, is only possible as a stable system if the population is stationary or nearly so. A slow increase might be coped with by improvements in agricultural methods, but a rapid increase must in the end reduce the whole population to penury, and would be almost certain to cause wars. In view of the fact that the population of France has become stationary, and that the birth-rate has declined enormously among other white nations, it may be hoped that the white population of the world will soon cease to increase. The Asiatic races will be longer, and the negroes still longer, before their birth-rate falls sufficiently to make their numbers stable without the help of war and pestilence. But it is to be hoped that the religious prejudices which have hitherto hampered the spread of birth control will die out, and that within (say) two hundred years the whole world will learn not to be unduly prolific. Until that happens, the benefits aimed at by socialism can only be partially realized, and the less prolific races will have to defend themselves against the more prolific by methods which are disgusting even if they are necessary. In the meantime, therefore, our socialistic aspirations have to be confined to the white races, perhaps with the inclusion of the Japanese and Chinese at no distant date.

Assuming such an organized framework for the material side of life, would it be possible to preserve mental freedom ? Or would those who controlled the economic organization use their power to persecute any set of people whose opinions or behaviour they happened to dislike ? I think it must be taken as perfectly certain that the officials in charge of rationing would wish to use their power to crush out all originality and all mental or moral progress. They would have an outlook not unlike that of employers of labour at present. If their power were unchecked, I do not doubt that they would kill art and science and every kind of free speculation about life and the world.

Let us take a few concrete illustrations. What would be done with a female school-teacher convicted of unchastity ? Or with a literary man convicted of writing in favour of a return to capitalism ? Or with a man who spent his leisure preaching Mormonism ? It is said—I do not vouch for the assertion—that the Bolsheviks prohibited the teaching of Einstein's doctrines on the ground that they undermined men's faith in the reality of matter. Even if this incident never occurred, similar interferences with science would certainly be attempted under State socialism. When I returned from China and was looking out for somewhere to live, I found a flat that suited me, and the tenant was willing to sub-let to me. But the superior landlord refused permission on the ground that he disliked my politics. After some correspondence, he offered to admit me at an exorbitant rent, provided I could get three householders to promise that I would abstain from political propaganda while the lease lasted. The existence of other landlords saved me from serious embarrassment, but if all houses had belonged to the State I might have been compelled to live abroad.

If the State has control of the land and of the food supply, the use of its economic power will have all the force at present belonging to the criminal law. A person whom the State is not willing to accept as a tenant, or to whom it refuses food tickets, will suffer as much as a convicted felon suffers at present. Therefore, unless there is to be an intolerable tyranny, the State's economic power will have to be hedged about by the same kind of safeguards that apply at present to police power. That is to say, the State must only exercise its economic power after establishing in a Law Court, or some *ad hoc* tribunal, a ground recognized as sufficient by the criminal law. To secure that this shall be legally required, public opinion will need to be alive to the dangers of bureaucracy, and trade unions will have to view State officials with the same kind of suspicion with which they now view employers. Organizations prepared to combat officials in the cause of liberty will be indispensable ; but if they exist and are active, there is no reason why liberty should not be preserved.

There are difficulties connected with the need of an incentive to work. Many men, no doubt, would work for the sake of the good opinion of others, or in order to rise to positions of power. But others will need stronger incentives. Assuming that everybody receives more than bare necessaries, the economic motive can still be used : a man who is incurably lazy or grossly negligent could be deprived of tobacco or alcohol or meat, or in some other way submitted to economic loss. Possibly in extreme cases prison might be necessary ; at any rate, the Bolsheviks found it so. The difficulty which arises is that the authorities in charge of a factory or workshop will be the only people competent to judge whether a man is shirking, and yet, if their judgment is accepted, he may be subject to personal persecution on account of some private grudge or on some wholly inadequate ground. In the case of a man who is unpopular among his comrades it seems impossible to devise any safeguard against injustice of this sort ; but in all ordinary cases, given self-government in industry, the public opinion of comrades is capable of affording protection against victimization.

It should be open to a man not to work for the State if he could get any group of people to support him out of their surplus. Artists, authors, editors of newspapers, and others whose work makes only a sectional appeal would come under this head.

From these considerations it is clear that the preservation of mental freedom under any form of socialism will require certain conditions. There must be an overwhelming public opinion against allowing the State, *qua* employer, to take any account of any-thing done outside working-hours, unless it has relevance to work, as in a case of revealing official secrets, for example. If a man commits a crime, he must be dealt with by the machinery of the law, but not by the economic machinery of the State. *Qua* employer, the State must take account of nothing but a man's efficiency in his work ; his opinions, his morals, and the general nature of his activities outside working-hours must be entirely ignored. This is not an impossible ideal ; it is one which the trade unions could easily enforce.

To diminish the uniformity of the official spirit, there must be as much self-government in industry as possible. The State must determine prices, though it will have to do so after bargaining with the industry ; it must also, of course, determine how much it needs of any commodity. By the simple device of leaving young people free to choose their trade or profession, the desirability of different occupations can be kept pretty nearly equal. This cannot be secured merely by equality of pay or of hours, because some occupations are more arduous or more disagreeable than others. The internal organization and administration of an industry should be left in its hands, and not interfered with by the State except on rare occasions when some crying scandal demanded attention.

What are the advantages to be hoped from such a system ?

In the first place, there would be an end of economic competition, bringing with it an almost total cessation of the motives for war. With the ending of competition there would no longer be any motive for the ruinous and spendthrift exploitation of natural resources which now goes on ; there would not be the vast development of advertisement and degraded cunning in marketing ; there would not be the present morality of success, with its ruthlessness and hypnotic propaganda. Gradually men's characters would change as they ceased to be obliged to stand on each other's shoulders. One might hope to see in time among western nations something of that urbanity and calm courtesy that characterizes Chinese literati and makes Chinese life delightful. There would cease also to be that all-pervading snobbery that makes everyone except the very poorest waste money in ostentation to impress neighbours—for instance, in a fine funeral. And there would no longer be the ever-present fear of destitution, which now haunts millions and makes them without scruple in the struggle for life.

With these changes there would come a quieter manner of life—less fever and hustle, fewer material changes, more leisure for meditation, less cleverness and more wisdom. At present, respect is secured by wealth ; in a society where wealth was unobtainable and poverty not to be feared, less material standards would prevail. A man would be respected for being a " good fellow," kindly, genial, or witty. Intellect and artistic ability would no longer be overshadowed by business skill, and would not have to sell themselves to gross millionaires. In such an atmosphere, art might revive and science might cease to be prostituted to commerce and war. The human spirit, freed at last from its immemorial bondage to material cares, might display fully for the first time all the splendour of which it is capable. Life might be happy for all, and intoxicatingly glorious for the best.

What stands in the way ? Greed, the lust of power, and the tyranny of custom. Perhaps, in the horror of the coming years, something of this dross may be purged from our nature, and we may learn to hope as the only alternative to despair. If so, the dark time through which the world is passing will not have been endured in vain.

INDEX

Printed in Great Britain by
UNWIN BROTHERS, LIMITED
LONDON AND WOKING

International Aspects of Unemployment

By Prof. WATSON KIRKCONNELL, M.A.

University of Manitoba

Cr. 8vo.   *6s. 6d.*

No problem to-day has greater significance than unemployment. This book by a Canadian publicist treats the phenomenon as an index to disharmonies and hazards in our whole international civilization. A vigorous premonitory plea for world co-operation.

The Economics of Unemployment
By J. A. HOBSON

Cr. 8vo.   *4s. 6d.*

"Combines once more the rare virtues of conciseness, clearness and authority. . . . The book demands, by the clearness of its exposition and the persuasiveness of its argument, the careful attention of everyone concerned over the serious problem with which it deals."—*Manchester Guardian.*

The Decay of Capitalist Civilisation

By SIDNEY AND BEATRICE WEBB

Cr. 8vo.   *Cloth, 4s. 6d. ; Paper, 2s. 6d.*

"Every Socialist will want to thank them for this book."—*New Leader.*
"The case against Capitalist Civilisation is argued with great cogency and wealth of illustrations."—*Observer.*

Stabilisation

An Economic Policy for Producers and Consumers

By E. M. H. LLOYD

Cr. 8vo. 4s. 6d.

" A book that everyone concerned in finding the solution of the present chaos in trade and industry should study carefully."—*Outlook.*

The League of Nations
To-day
Its Growth, Record and Relation to British Foreign Policy

Cr. 8vo. By ROTH WILLIAMS 6s.

This book aims to give an authoritative presentment of the existing League as an instrument issued from the play of certain kinds of public opinion and foreign policy during the last few years, and makes concrete suggestions for the perfection and use of this instrument in readjusting the relations between Great Britain and the Dominions and Great Britain, India and Egypt; for inducing America to co-operate with Europe; for achieving full political and financial settlement between the Allies and Germany and Russia; and for the civilization of patriotism.

War : Its Nature, Cause and
Cure
By G. LOWES DICKINSON
Author of "The Choice before Us," etc.

Cr. 8vo. 4s. 6d.

This is a book of propaganda addressed to the plain man. It shows that war with modern weapons cannot be waged on a great scale without destroying civilization and mankind. It shows also that the real causes of war are always the desires of some states, or of all states, to steal territory, markets and concessions. It analyses, in this sense, the causes of the late war. And it appeals to the ordinary citizen to come out on the side of ending war if he wants to prevent the ending of mankind.

Towards International Justice

By F. N. KEEN

Barrister-at-Law

WITH AN INTRODUCTION BY PROF. GILBERT MURRAY

Cr. 8vo.   *7s. 6d.*

The principles underlying the League of Nations are discussed and its constitution and machinery described. Practical suggestions are made for the fuller development of the League on lines of justice and international law. The author was a pioneer in the League of Nations movement and is on the Executive Committee of the League of Nations Union.

Political Crime

By W. G. CARLTON HALL

Barrister-at-Law

Cr. 8vo.   *4s. 6d.*

The author here attempts to explain the failure of the British Government in recent times to deal effectively with the growing tendency to use violence in the pursuit of political or revolutionary aims. The first part consists of a statement, in text-book form, of the existing law in relation to this class of crime, and among the other subjects dealt with are the willingness of the Legislature to weaken that law from time to time; the contrasting practice of both Legislature and Executive in resorting to emergency measures in time of war or civil disturbance (including therein the proclamation and exercise of martial law); and the common habit of the Executive to mitigate or remit sentences passed by the Courts in respect of " political " offences.

The Saar Question

A Disease Spot in Europe

By SIDNEY OSBORNE

Demy 8vo.   *12s. 6d.*

This is a discussion of the Saar Settlement under the Treaty of Versailles and an examination of the results attained thereby down to the present. The important bearing of the problem upon future world peace in view of the misuse of the powers granted by the League of Nations, as Trustee, to its agents, the Governing Commission of the Saar Basin, is minutely dealt with. The book is very fully documented.

China in The Family of Nations

By Dr. HENRY T. HODGKIN
Author of "The Christian Revolution," "Lay Religion," etc.

Cr. 8vo.   *6s. 6d.*

After reviewing the history of China in her international relationships, the author (who has had some twenty years' intimate and varied experience of the country) attempts to show what the result means for China herself and for the rest of mankind. He discusses the international situation, the industrial development of China and the New Thought Movement, and seeks throughout to present the case for China in a sympathetic way.

The Problem of China

By BERTRAND RUSSELL, F.R.S.

La. Cr. 8vo.   *7s. 6d.*

" Few have brought to their task a more exquisite sensitiveness or a swifter, stronger understanding."—*Daily Herald.*

"A stimulating contribution to our understanding of these Oriental forms of civilization."—*Times.*

The Far Eastern Republic of Siberia

By HENRY KITTREDGE NORTON

Demy 8vo.   *12s. 6d.*

This is the first unbiassed and authoritative account of what has been happening during the last four years in the Far Eastern portion of the former Russian Empire. The author is the only foreign traveller who has been through all the territory from Lake Baikal to the Pacific since the Allied troops were withdrawn. Penetrating the wall of propaganda which has been built about this part of the world, he lived many months with the Russians of the Far East. The result is this book—a fascinating description of the struggle of the peasants for independence and self-government.

All prices net.

LONDON : GEORGE ALLEN & UNWIN LIMITED
RUSKIN HOUSE, 40 MUSEUM STREET, W.C. 1